Essential Tips to Avoid Property Taxes

Essential
Tips to Avoid
Property Taxes

What's George up to?

Helping you make sense of the tax changes

to increase your wealth

Iain Wallis

ISBN 978-1530959-112

Disclaimer

This is a book aimed at providing tax tips for those of you who like me choose to invest in property and is intended for general guidance only.

It does not constitute accountancy, tax, financial or other professional advice.

The author makes no representations or warranties with regard to the accuracy or completeness of this book and cannot accept any responsibility for any liability, loss or risk, personal or otherwise which may arise, directly or indirectly, from reliance on information contained in this book.

This book completed in April 2016 reflects current UK tax legislation the current law and practices of the government and HMRC though these are constantly changing and may have changed when you read this book.

Please note that your personal circumstances may vary from the generic information contained within this book and the examples given and thus may not be suitable for you or your family. It is therefore essential that for accountancy, tax, financial or other professional advice you seek professional advice specific to your circumstances.

This book deals solely with UK taxation, which for tax purposes excludes the Isle of Man and The Channel Islands. Nor is this a book about the taxation in foreign countries.

Writing a book is quite a daunting task! For making sure that it's friendly on the eye and free of minsprits I'm very grateful to Jacqueline Campbell at www.virtual-angel.co.uk

About the author

Iain had an early introduction to business life when his late father started his own manufacturing company.

As a teenager it was a great introduction to the world of business and though he became increasingly interested in the business, his father had no desire for him to join it citing the mantra "Father, Son, Bankrupt", so on leaving university, he trained and qualified as a Chartered Accountant in 1984.

He started his own accountancy practice in 1992, developed it and eventually sold it in 2007.

Iain bought his first investment property in 2006 and has continued since then to acquire property for himself and other investors. After an adult gap year or two, too young to retire, Iain realised that there was a need to help the increasing band of seasoned property investors who were paying too much tax.

Building on his experience of over 30 year as a Chartered Accountant helping clients like the readers of this book, and with all his property investing knowledge, he has created a niche accountancy and tax practice that deals solely with high net worth individuals; it delivers sound taxation advice and legal tax strategies that avoid, and thus save, thousands of pounds in tax.

Iain's first book Legally Avoid Property Taxes: 51 Top Tips to Save property taxes and improve your wealth is a Number 1 Amazon Best Seller.

Iain is also a powerful and entertaining keynote speaker, and uses practical day-to-day examples to explain away the complexities of taxation – and, in particular, property taxation. He prides himself on his down-to-earth manner – and the ability to make saving tax fun. Iain engages his audience with humour, whilst at the same time delivering tax strategies that can save thousands and, in some cases, millions of pounds.

Iain was a keynote speaker at the largest property event in the property calendar, The Property Super Conference 2013 at Wembley, London, where he shared the stage with some of the best-known property experts in the UK, as well as high-profile speakers such as Karren Brady and Frank Bruno. Iain's presentation *Legally Keep More of Your Property Income* was a sell-out – it must be the first time Wembley has rocked to tax!

It's not all about property though. Although not a native until 2008, he lives in the county of Northumberland: close to glorious beaches and the hills of the Cheviots. A lifelong – and sometimes long-suffering – supporter of all sport played by England, Iain, along with his wife Fenella, had the good fortune to be in Sydney in 2003 to see England win the Rugby World Cup.

This is the one.
It's coming back to Jonny Wilkinson.
He drops for World Cup Glory.
He's done it, it's over.
Wilkinson is England's hero yet again and there's no time for Australia to come back.
England have just won the Rugby World Cup".

The immortal words of BBC Commentator, Ian Robertson.

On the 22nd November 2003, Iain and Fenella saw that wonderful event in Sydney as, after a three-week rugby holiday, they watched England win the rugby World Cup. "It was one of the best and happiest days in our life together," recounts Iain. As England went from inept to incompetent in 2015 we could at least console ourselves with the fact that we used to be good at yet another sport that we invented!

On 5th December 2003, Fenella's sister Davina lost her brave battle against cancer, the saddest day in their lives. This was not supposed to happen. Davina had done well through all the treatments and, with her deep faith, was well on the way to recovery. Little did they all realise how savage the cancer was. It returned with a vengeance.

Talk about 14 days of contrasting emotions and, yes, a reality check.

She was the same age as Iain, just 46, and left three wonderful children, a husband and a close family. So, please: follow Iain, and enjoy life, live every day as if it could be your last and, like Iain, give whatever you can, whenever you can, to Cancer Research.

Please note that £1 of the purchase price of this book will be given to Cancer Research.

A note about the examples

Throughout this book where possible I have used worked examples to facilitate explanation of the tax tip. For the avoidance of doubt, unless specifically stated all persons used for examples are UK resident, ordinarily resident and domiciled for tax purposes.

Where rates and amounts will change I have included hyperlinks to the HMRC website to allow you to have up-to-date information. That said, tax law and interpretations of it can, and does change overnight; you should bear this in mind when applying examples to your real-life situations.

Unless specifically indicated otherwise, all persons used in the examples in this book are entirely fictional created simply to facilitate the explanation of the tax tips. Any similarities to actual persons, living or dead are entirely coincidental.

As you work your way through you will see a theme developing from the names used in examples and I trust that my knowledge and love for the British & Irish Lions has ensured an equal representation.

Contents

Chapter 1

Introduction

One of the challenges about writing a book on tax is that tax law and the interpretation of it can, and does change overnight. There was thus a certain crossing of the fingers when I finally signed off my first book "Legally Avoid Property Taxes: 51 Top tips to save property taxes and increase your wealth", a book that was to become a number one best seller on Amazon, to go to the printers.

Sure I expected there to be annual changes in the banding at which different rates of tax apply and with a fair wind increases in the personal allowance i.e. the amount that everyone can earn before the impact of taxation and for that very reason hyperlinks were included where relevant. The book was deliberately generic talking about principles and strategies that people who like me chose to invest in property can apply to legally avoid property taxes and retain more of their wealth. That said many of the examples need updating for 2016, so still plenty of keyboard work required.

Until July 2015 I'm pleased to say that though there were the predicted changes in bandings, personal allowances etc. there had been only two significant changes namely a change to the rates in stamp duty and the reduction to 18 months of deemed ownership when you sell a property that was once your main residence. One technical change, which is very much to our advantage and this along with the two points above will be addressed within this book.

So, some two years after the book was released it continues to sell well and I'm always delighted to receive a quarterly royalty payment for the printed version and a monthly one for the EBook and pleased to know that I'm among the 5% that have sold more than 5,000 copies of the 195,000 books published in a year. Plus it has that much coveted Amazon Number 1 bestseller. Incidentally, that has been achieved through sales at market value and not through some 48 hour promotional fire sale where the book is sold for a pound and a favourable review in an attempt to fool the Amazon algorithms into thinking they have just unearthed the next George Clancy or JK Rowling!

So on July 8 2015 when the Chancellor produced his first Conservative majority budget I was expecting the usual inflationary adjustments to personal allowances, the delivery of a few election promises and maybe a couple of pence on a pint!

I think it's fair to say he caught a lot of us by surprise with the sweeping changes that he's now making to the buy to let sector and George Osborne bless him overnight became Head of my Marketing Department.

Us property investors are clearly in the Chancellors sites with the abolition of the 10% wear and tear allowance, restrictions to the tax relief available on loan interest, changes to dividend taxation, though there was some help on Inheritance Tax though just how much of that was an election sop? I have to confess that when Ed Balls lost his seat at the general election I thought that were on our way to electing a Conservative government!

Cue thousands of words about the injustice of it all, how investors pay capital gains tax, how we help the chronic housing shortage in the UK and I guess I'm adding to this with this book.

Facts are they've moved the goal posts and writing as an investor myself I would say unfairly and this is backed up by economists and commentators.

On the 9th of July, the day after the budget, Paul Johnson, Director of the impartial Institute for Fiscal Studies said: *'At present if you own a property which you let out to tenants you can set any mortgage interest costs against tax due on rent received. The Budget red book states that this means that 'the current tax system supports landlords over and above ordinary homeowners,' and that it 'puts investing in a rental property at an advantage.'* This line of argument is plain wrong. Rental property is taxed more heavily than owner occupied property.

Source:http://www.ifs.org.uk/uploads/publications/budgets/Budgets%202015/Summer/opening_remarks.pdf

The think tank, Policy Exchange, notes that "the tax system massively favours home ownership – for one thing home owners do not have to pay capital gains tax on their principal residence, whereas buy to let landlords do on the rental properties they sell. Rental income is also taxed".

Source:http://www.policyexchange.org.uk/media-centre/blogs/category/item/ additional-policy-exchange-analysis-of-summer-budget-2015

The July 2015 Budget was then followed with the Autumn statement and the 3% hike in Stamp Duty Land tax for additional property purchases (the final details of which were only announced in the Budget on 16 March 2016) and some of you may have been caught in the mad panic to complete a purchase before 31 March 2016.

For all the noise and petitions I can't see them having much impact and getting the Chancellor to change his mind. Even crossing Cherie Blaire's palm with silver and a potential Judicial Review is in my view unlikely to succeed and even if it did old George would just move the goal posts. So how we deal with these significant changes as with anything in life, will determine our success as property investors. For some there will be massive short term pain that may require a complete review of why they invest in property, but through that pain may come clarity and long term gain; some part time landlords may choose to exit the market and for others a bit of tweaking will be all that is required.

Don't get me wrong I'm not making light of these changes, though David Gauke, financial secretary to the Treasury, estimates that only one landlord in five is expected to pay more tax. My question to you therefore is what can you do to ensure that you are not the one of those five?

The important thing as Corporal Jones told us frequently is "Don't Panic".

The most draconian change is the removal of interest tax relief at higher rates of tax, Clause 24, but we've a few years to get our house or more likely our portfolio in order before that impacts in full. Mr Gauke, bless him, helpfully tells us that this restriction will be phased in over four years beginning on 6 April 2017 in recognition of the "hardworking people who have saved and invested in property" and thus depend on property income. How very thoughtful, though as I will demonstrate in this book all is not lost.

Take stock of where you are, what you want to achieve and move forward. We're in business and yes we face challenges so let's tackle those head on and from this book you will find something that works for you. As always there is never a one size fits all solution; people invest for many different reasons, have different income streams and even exit strategies.

That said I've massive sympathy for one group of people. Since April 2015, over-55s have been allowed to cash in their pensions and spend it as they wish rather than being forced to buy an annuity to provide a regular income for life. This has led to a rise in people using their savings to buy a second property, which fell out of favour following the financial crisis when property prices plummeted. Those who've been encouraged to take cash from their pension now find that their single buy to let property may not produce quite the income they thought it would, but again all is not lost. I really don't buy the view that these changes weren't planned and it seems very underhand.

It will do no harm to remind you of one of the main drivers behind writing the first book.

Imagine having to write a cheque to the Inland Revenue for £1.8 million. Can you feel the pain? Can you see how many noughts that is? Can you imagine the joy of the taxman?

Do you feel sick to know that that that tax revenue will go to pay the benefits of those who chose not to work in our society?

What could your children or grandchildren have done with that money?

Now imagine that, instead of writing a cheque for £1.8 million, you had written a cheque for £360,000 – making a saving of £1,440,000! How good does that feel?

What could you have done with all that extra money? How would that have helped your life? Would that have enabled you to secure the future for your children or even your grandchildren?

And the sad thing is that this actually happened to a UK taxpayer. She had been using a non-specialist property tax accountant who, each year, had happily prepared her returns and collected a fee without thinking about what might happen one day. She was diagnosed with an illness that left her with less than a year to live. Suddenly minds were concentrated and her daughter, after frantic checking on the Internet, found and approached me wanting to know if I could help with a massive Inheritance Tax problem.

The answer, of course, was yes. Steps were put in place, even with such a short lifespan, to help keep the money away from the taxman.

Alas, the illness was worse than initially diagnosed and she died within two weeks of our initial meeting. So the Inland Revenue picked up a very nice cheque.

You don't want to be the next person to write out another large cheque to HMRC do you?

Inheritance Tax is just one of many taxes that can potentially take a significant chunk out of your hard-earned income from property. Whilst in this case a lot of the wealth had come from property inflation, it was wealth nonetheless; wealth that should be passed through the generations, not – in my humble opinion – passed across to the Treasury.

So why write this book and just who is it for?

First out let me say that this is not a tax manual. I'm sure that you have no difficulty dropping off to sleep at night. Wherever you are in your property journey, this is a book for you.

This book builds on the fifty-one tax tips that you should be aware of to legally avoid tax – whether you do your own self-assessment returns or pass everything over to your accountant. I want to make absolutely sure that you've not left any money on the HMRC table.

So, this is not a rewrite or an update of the Amazon Best Seller available here www.iainwallis.com/booksale. More it's a review of what significant changes have been brought about by the 2015 Budget, how you can make sense of these changes and what you can do to lessen the impact of direct taxation on your property portfolio. That said, I'm working on an expanded and updated version of the original book to be published later this year.

Believe me when I say that the 2015 budget, wherever you are on your property journey, has made changes that will impact on you and I want to make sure that you don't just stumble across them. Armed with the correct knowledge, they can be dealt with.
I want you to be aware of the pain that taxation can cause you – because when you are aware of that pain you take action. But then you knew that anyway, didn't you?

To *avoid* tax requires careful planning but, above all, it requires you to take action.

As a mentor of mine says "to know and not to do is not to know"!

So read through this in its entirety – or dip in where you want to if you have a specific query.

You will find stuff that you can apply, take action and above all legally avoid tax.

Chapter two sees a healthy debate about tax and tax avoidance and the rights and wrongs.

Chapter three will highlight the tax changes to consider.

Chapter four will look at the buy to let income changes.

Chapter five will drill down further into how to deal with those changes.

Chapter six will deal with dividend changes.

Chapter seven will look at the bigger picture of Inheritance Tax.

Chapter eight takes a look at the introduction of Residence Nil Rate Band (RNRB).

Above all, please enjoy: Moira Stuart and Adam Hart-Davies are not wrong when they say "tax doesn't have to be taxing"!

Chapter 2

Tax Avoidance or Tax Evasion

2.1 Introduction

There continues to be much talk about tax avoidance and tax evasion. So it will do no harm to remind you, the reader, of the difference between the two. With the changes being introduced it's vital that you stay on the right side of the law.

Lord Clyde famously said, in the case of Ayrshire Pullman Motor Services v IRC 14 TC 754 (1929): No man in this country is under the smallest obligation, moral or other, so to arrange his legal relations to his business or to his property as to enable the Inland Revenue to put the largest possible shovel into his stores. The Inland Revenue is not slow, and quite rightly, to take every advantage which is open to it under the taxing statutes for the purpose of depleting the taxpayer's pocket. And the taxpayer is, in like manner, entitled to be astute to prevent, so far as he honestly can, the depletion of his means by the Revenue.

From where I'm sitting, which is actually overlooking the Swiss Alps writing this book, that is game on and we as taxpayers should do all we can to pay the right amount of tax but not a penny more than we have to.

2.2 Avoidance

So let's nail this thing about tax avoidance right at the start.

Her Majesty's Revenue & Customs or, indeed, the Chancellor of the Exchequer may not like tax avoidance – but it is perfectly legal. Let me repeat that, because it is so important: *Tax avoidance is perfectly legal.*

It is well-established that you can manage your affairs to legitimately avoid tax. So what if the actions that you take mean that you gain and the taxman misses out. Do you really want to pay more tax? Are you serious?

Ignorance is not bliss in life and certainly not with tax! Not knowing how you can *legitimately* avoid tax, or being scared of the taxman, is restricting and damaging your personal wealth.

You have a responsibility to yourself, to your spouse or partner, your children and grandchildren to take charge of these matters to maximise your personal wealth.

Everything in this book is completely legal, safe to apply and should be being used by accountants up and down the land. If your accountant is not, then you genuinely have the wrong accountant. I continue to field calls from people who aren't convinced that their accountant is up to speed on property tax issues. I would not go to a dentist to get my heart looked at, nor would I expect a heart surgeon to be particularly good at sorting wisdom teeth. So please appoint a specialist and by that it must be an accountant who specialises in property and dare I say it has a few properties themselves.

Ask yourself this key question: is your accountant an undercover agent for HMRC?

In terms of risk, where 1 is looking both ways before you cross the road and then checking again, to 10 where you are smacking a wasps' nest, these are all in the 1-2 range. There are some very aggressive tax schemes out there, but they are not for this book.

Jimmy Carr, amongst others, found himself in hot water for following such an aggressive scheme. But wait. He has done nothing wrong. Controversial maybe, but all he's done is legally avoided tax.

Now some of us may not like that, and it is for his moral compass to decide if he is happy with his decisions – but he has taken that choice through advice from his accountant and professional advisors. His advisors would be failing in their professional duty if they did not present these opportunities to him.

So please, please bury – no, not bury, smash the belief that tax avoidance is illegal.

Smash it into thousands of little pieces.

That said, every accountant is taught at a very early age: "Don't let the tax tail wag the dog!" An action taken may save a load of tax – but does that action really make commercial sense in your specific case? Is it really worth the effort, or the risk, or the expense? Don't spend a pound to save a penny! So please bear that in mind as you make your way through this book.

Aggressive schemes pursued by companies or highly paid entertainers may not sit with your moral compass – but it has never been, and never will be, illegal to manage your affairs to avoid tax.
Increasingly these particularly aggressive schemes are being targeted, so let HMRC and the Chancellor worry about them and you put your own house in order,

Ah, you may say. That's all well and good, but everywhere I turn I'm told that tax avoidance is wrong. So why are we being brainwashed into believing that tax avoidance is a problem for everyone?

Her Majesty's Revenue & Customs, (from now, simply 'HMRC') and HM Treasury have a shared objective of minimising the tax gap. The tax gap is the difference between the tax collected and the tax which

HMRC think ought to be collected. In addition, you might have spotted that UK Plc is a little short of funds at the moment and finding novel ways to try and balance the books!

To quote from the HMRC website:

We want to provide our customers with a level playing field, while maintaining the UK's international competitiveness. Our strategy for delivering this objective is through encouraging everyone to pay tax at the right time and vigorously tackling those who deliberately avoid their responsibilities.

It continues:

In the UK, the tax loss from avoidance is estimated to run into several billion pounds across both direct and indirect taxes...

(Direct taxes are taxes that individuals or companies pay direct to HMRC, such as Income Tax, Corporation Tax or National Insurance, whereas indirect taxes are charged on goods and services, such as excise duty, insurance tax and VAT.)

This directly affects the delivery of public services and long-term economic growth. Avoidance distorts markets, is economically unproductive and breaks the link between economic productivity and reward.

Helpfully it tells us that:

The vast majority of our customers do not participate in tax avoidance and will stand to benefit from HMRC's anti-avoidance strategy. HMRC is taking a proportionate, risk-based approach to avoidance, which is consistent with HMRC's commitment to supporting our customers.

Isn't it just wonderful that we taxpayers are now seen as customers; maybe, one day, HMRC will discover the concept of customer service and deliver a great experience? As agents to taxpayers we get a dedicated line, but have you as a 'customer' ever called them on the phone? If you do have to, be sure to arm yourself with a cup of coffee and prepare for a long wait.

The phone lines are the only way you can contact HMRC after they closed most of their offices and with a digital system which is still in development, they remain a lifeline if you need to sort out your tax affairs, so the telephone system has to work.

'Waiting times are not uncommonly over half an hour. This can be very expensive for those on pay-as-you-go. The '0300' number to call the taxman is typically 9p a minute from landlines and between 8p and 40p a minute from mobiles, unless the user has a free calls package, according to Ofcom estimates.

Between April 2014 and March 2015, 64.7million calls were made to HMRC, of which 72 per cent (46.8million) were successfully answered. This fell short of the revenue body's target of 80 per cent. Imagine running business where you only answered 72% of your incoming calls and yet HMRC get away with it!

Less helpfully, they tell us that *"it is impossible to provide a comprehensive definition of avoidance"* and thus it is, therefore, impossible for them to give any guidance to us poor impoverished taxpayers as to how they plan to "level this playing field".

So relax.

Don't you worry about our international competitiveness! Concentrate instead on doing what you can do to ensure that, where possible, you follow every tip in this book to legally – and without fear or remorse – avoid tax and thus reduce your tax bill.

2.3   General Anti-Abuse Rules (GAAR)

Just to add to the mix, since April 2013 the long-awaited and much-talked-about general anti-abuse rules came into force.

The first thing to say is that this is not, as widely feared, a green flag for HMRC to ride roughshod over anything it didn't like. Fortunately for us humble taxpayers nothing has really changed. It is more aimed at egregious tax planning and schemes for those with a far higher risk profile to tax planning and schemes that are not covered in this book.

The general message is that *avoiding* tax, by making the most of the tax rules, is OK! However, taking steps that are *artificial or abnormal*, or which are *solely to escape tax* will fall foul of GAAR. In those circumstances HMRC will claw back the tax saved and, as ever, help themselves to penalties.

The only issue now is that what *you* consider to be fair avoidance might be different from HMRC; rather unhelpfully, there is no system to ask HMRC in advance if your proposed action will be acceptable under GAAR, or will fall foul of the rules.
Helpfully for us property investors, it specifically gives examples of 'flipping' and giving assets to your children to avoid taxes. These are acceptable actions as to the making use of current tax law; having waded through the guide it's safe to say that GAAR should not impact on those making the most of the available rules.

Tax *evasion,* however, is completely different – so, as M, would say "Pay attention, 007!"

2.4　Evasion

Whilst legitimate tax avoidance is legal and to be encouraged at all times, evasion is not legal and certainly not to be encouraged.

Put simply, tax evasion happens when people deliberately don't pay the tax they should. Tax evasion is a crime and everyone loses out because of it. Naturally, HMRC is committed to tackling tax evasion.

Before all the doom and gloom, it is important to point out that the law does not require perfection. It requires that you take 'reasonable care' to get your tax right. We are now, and have been for a number of years, under self-assessment; it is for you to provide all the information and get your tax right.

If you make a genuine mistake and can demonstrate that you took 'reasonable care' no penalty will be due.

Alas, there is no legal definition of 'reasonable care' so common sense will prevail and the facts of each case.

If you "forgot" that you sold a property and didn't declare a capital gain that's hardly reasonable care and most likely tax evasion!

If, in the absence of a lost bill, you over-estimated some capital improvement costs when completing your tax return which was found to be excessive then you are unlikely to unleash the Harbingers of Hell at HMRC.

The three things to consider are:

- Have you under-declared your tax liability?
- Have you over-claimed tax repayments?
- Have you failed to tell them that you are liable to pay tax?

At its worst, tax evasion could find you serving time at Her Majesty's pleasure; while you will be guaranteed three square meals and a bed for the night it doesn't look too good on the CV! There are the high-profile cases of Lester Piggott (who was jailed for three years for tax evasion and stripped of his OBE) but it also happens to ordinary people.

Landlords and property investors need to be aware of the tax office's (HMRC) increasing focused, intelligence based and assertive approach to tax investigations. A significant investment in IT, better use of evaluating the immense amount of data accessible by HMRC (such as Land Registry documents, letting agents records, council tax records), additional HMRC staff, significant penalties for 'non-declarers', wider media exposure and more use of the criminal courts significantly increases the likelihood of being investigated by the big beast that is HMRC.

It is believed that HMRC knows exactly how many owners are trying to sell which investment properties, their primary source of information is now becoming the internet which produces high grade information, not only of houses for sale or to rent but also of planning applications in relation to proposed house conversions which are then sold at a later date producing a potential Capital Gains Tax liability. Increasingly letting agents are being asked for the client list so that HMRC can check that the rental income is being declared.

As you will see in this book there are more than enough *legitimate* ways to avoid tax. So please, please, do not go down the evasion route.

Evasion means worrying every time you get a phone call from an unusual number, worrying about that knock on the door at some unearthly hour, and constantly being on edge. Life's far too short for that.

So please *avoid* – but don't *evade*!

As that annoying little rodent says, "Simples!"

Chapter 3

Tax Changes to Consider

3.1   Stamp Duty Land Tax (SDLT)

This tax is payable when there is a transfer of property or land In England, Wales and Northern Ireland over a certain price or consideration. The current SDLT threshold is £125,000 for residential property and £150,000 for non-residential land and property. Note that SDLT no longer applies in Scotland where you will now pay a Land & Buildings Transaction tax. Whichever vehicle you choose to trade through, sole trader, company partnership, and whether you are a property developer or a property investor, then the same rates will apply – in virtually all circumstances.

You pay the tax when you:

- buy a freehold property
- buy a new or existing leasehold
- buy a property through a shared ownership scheme
- are transferred land or property in exchange for payment, eg you take on a mortgage or buy a share in a house (think transfers between spouses)

The total value you pay SDLT on (sometimes called the 'consideration') is usually the price you pay for the property or land.

Sometimes it might include another type of payment like:

- release from a debt
- transfer of a debt, including the value of any outstanding mortgage

You pay Stamp Duty Land Tax (SDLT) on increasing portions of the property price above £125,000 when you buy residential property, e.g a house or flat.

Purchase price/lease premium or transfer value	SDLT rate
Up to £150,000 - if annual rent is under £1,000	Zero
Up to £150,000 - if annual rent is £1,000 or more	1%
£150,001 to £250,000	1%
£250,001 to £500,000	3%
Over £500,000	4%

Example If you buy a house for £275,000, the SDLT you owe is calculated as follows:

- 0% on the first £125,000 = £0
- 2% on the next £125,000 = £2,500
- 5% on the final £25,000 = £1,250
- Total SDLT = £3,750

It's not a particularly pleasant tax and HMRC simply help themselves to your wealth simply because you choose to purchase a house. As can be seen above, the rates become quite penal and the amounts payable can be considerable.

The introduction of the sliding scale was designed to remove anomalies in how SDLT was applied. To give an extreme example under the old rules a house sold for £250,000 which would attract a duty of £2,500 (a flat 1% of the purchase price); but a house sold for just £1 more, at £250,001, would attract (if that's the word!) duty of £7,500, at 3%. So it would actually cost you £5,000 to pay one pound more for a property.

Under the new rules, that SDLT charge for offering an extra pound to secure the property would now only be 5p and not such a deal breaker!

Whilst kindly removing the fixed bands George did away with the initial 1% rate and whereas the 5% rate used to kick in at properties over a million that now comes in at houses over £675,000.

3.1.1 The 3% Surcharge

From 1 April, 2016 you'll have to pay a staggering extra 3% in Stamp Duty if you are buying a second home.

What this means is that those lovely high yielding investment properties below £125,000 will now attract Stamp Duty as can be seen in the table below.

Band	Existing residential SDLT rates	New additional property SDLT rates
£0 - £125k	0%	3%
£125k - £250k	2%	5%
£250k - £925k	5%	8%
£925k - £1.5m	10%	13%
£1.5m +	12%	15%

Anyone who is buying additional residential properties, for example a holiday home or buy-to-let, within England, Wales, Northern Ireland and - under a separate announcement in the Scottish Government's Budget - in Scotland too will be caught by this tax increase.

The surcharge will apply even if the home you already own (or part-own) is overseas. So, if you live and work overseas and are now buying your first home in the UK, you'd still be stung with the extra tax.

As indicated above, regular Stamp Duty is charged on a tiered basis (so you only pay the higher rate on the slice *above* any threshold – the same as income tax). But the 3% surcharge will still effectively work as a slab tax. In other words, the 3% loading will apply to the entire purchase price of the property.

Dallaglio is buying a second home with a purchase price of £300,000, so just the extra 3% Stamp Duty would equate to £9,000 (3% of the entire price). This is in addition to the £5,000 regular Stamp Duty bill on a home of this value, making the total payable an eye-watering £14,000.

If the home you are buying directly replaces your main residence, you will not be liable for the 3% surcharge, even if you own an additional home/s at the same time, but beware of a few nasty surprises.

Say you move out of your main residence (Home A) but keep it and buy another main residence (Home B), you will have to pay the 3% Stamp Duty surcharge initially. However, so long as you sell Home A within 36 months of completing on the purchase of Home B, HMRC will make a full refund. OK so you get the additional SDLT back but that will put considerable strain on your personal cashflow!

What about unmarried couples? Even if just one of you already owns a home, when you are buying another one together, the 3% Stamp Duty surcharge will apply.

If you are separated or getting divorced and want to buy a new home to live in, but your name is still on the deeds of the family home (which is NOT being sold), this will constitute buying an additional property which means the 3% surcharge will apply. However married couples who are living separately in circumstances that are likely to become permanent will NOT be treated as one unit for the purposes of the 3% surcharge. In other words, if you are buying a home that only incurs the 3% surcharge on the basis of your legal spouse's situation, you won't have to pay it.

At its simplest if the answer to any question is two, then the 3% SDLT will apply as can be seen below.

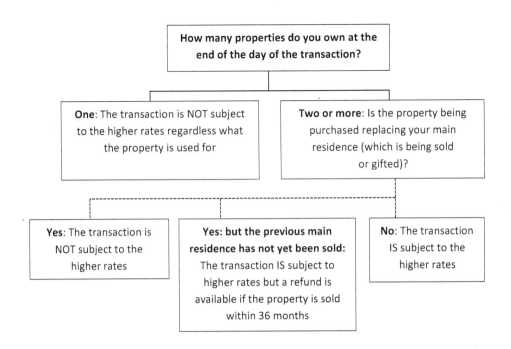

Now some of you might be thinking that I'll I just omit to mention to my solicitor about the fact I already have a home? Well please don't be so foolish as you are entering in to evasion territory and spookily HMRC has instructed the country's solicitors and property lawyers to ask buyers the question outright of whether they already own another property. If you don't answer truthfully it's tantamount to fraud - penalties for which could be a lot worse than a 3% Stamp Duty loading!

There is some good news though: you won't pay the 3% Stamp Duty surcharge on second homes that cost less than £40,000 and yes they do exist, but remember they are cheap for a reason, nor on caravans, mobile homes and houseboats if that was your choice of investment.

In addition social landlords and charities won't be charged the 3% loading. Please don't think that nipping in on a Sunday to check that your tenants are OK will make you a social landlord! Registered providers (often known as social landlords) are the bodies that own and manage social housing. They tend to be non-commercial organisations such as local authorities or housing associations.

So for landlords the 3% will bite but here's my take on it. Yes 3% is an a(
cost that needs to be factored in but written off over the length that you
property is it really such a deal breaker? Above all, as investors we make our ...money
when we buy, so brush up on your negotiating skills. Remember agents want to sell
houses to earn their commission, so build rapport with them and get them on your
side to help negotiate away that 3% hike with the vendors.

Finally, it's worth remembering that if you do decide to sell an investment property,
you can offset the cost of the 3% Stamp Duty surcharge when calculating the capital
gains tax liability.

A couple more things to be aware of regarding SDLT:

3.1.2.   Linked transactions

The "linked transactions" rule in effect prevents transactions being fragmented to
benefit from lower SDLT rates. Broadly, linked transactions are those made as part
of a single scheme or arrangement between the same seller and the same
purchaser.

Determining whether two or more transactions are linked is a question of fact
based on all of the surrounding circumstances. For example, it is likely that a series
of single transactions between the same seller and purchaser would be linked if
they were, in essence, part of the same deal or arrangements.

The period of time between the transactions is unlikely to be a material factor, but
if they take place within a relatively short period this often indicates that they are
part of the same deal.

From 4 December 2014, the SDLT on linked residential property transactions is
calculated by aggregating the separate consideration for each linked transaction.

The SDLT is then computed on the relevant consideration based on the principles
explained above.

ans being a property speculator is buying a new house from a builder. Now we all know that you don't buy new build because you are paying the builder his profit but stick with the example. Later, he buys a second and finally a third house. The builder offers a special price for the second and third houses. Being a sound negotiator Evans agrees a final price of £180,000 for each house once it's completed.

The three transactions link as part of a series. So initially we need to calculate the amount of tax due on the initial acquisition and then work out the total chargeable consideration for all the transactions to date, at the rates in force at the time of that transaction. This amount is then apportioned to each transaction in proportion to its share of the total chargeable consideration. Yes you've guessed it; he may have to pay some more tax on the earlier transaction(s).

Such confusion is worthy of an example:

On the first transaction, SDLT is due at 0% on £125,000 and 2% on £55,000 (£125,000 + £55,000 = £180,000 price of first house), total £1,100.

However on the second transaction the tax due on the total price of £360,000 (spookily £180,000 for two houses) is:

- 0% on £125,000
- 2% on £125,000
- 5% on £110,000

Total £8,000

At this stage the SDLT due on each transaction is £4,000, so an additional £2,900 is due for the earlier transaction.

On the third transaction the SDLT due on the total consideration of £540,000 (now £180,000 for three houses) is:

- 0% on £125,000
- 2% on £125,000
- 5% on £290,000

Total £17,000.

At this stage the tax due on each transaction is £5,666 (£17,000/3), so an additional £1,666 is due for each of the first and second transactions.

In an ideal world three houses each bought for £180,000 would produce a SDLT charge of £3,300.

Note that if each transaction in this example wasn't linked, the amount of SDLT payable on the second and third transactions would have been the same as on the first. So the total SDLT due on the 3 transactions would have been £3,300.

This could be the case if Evans had bought each of the 3 houses from the same builder in 3 completely separate transactions with:

- no prior agreement or option
- no special price or discount
- anything else to link them

So, by being clever and negotiating a prior agreement to buy at a special price Evans has potentially paid an additional £13,700. So care needs to be taken when structuring a deal and negotiating prices.

The example above is before the additional 3% applies! You will now know that Evans could potentially be looking at a further 3% on £180,000 three times!

That said there is a very useful relief where transactions include the acquisition of interests in more than one dwelling. Where the relief is claimed, the rate of SDLT which applies to the consideration attributable to interests in dwellings is determined by reference to the amount of this consideration, divided by the number of dwellings (i.e. the mean consideration attributable to the dwellings) or more snappily Multiple Dwellings Relief.

3.1.3 Multiple Dwellings Relief

Where several properties were acquired under the linked transactions rule, the Multiple Dwellings Relief or MDR (and no this is not something you can contract in a hospital) was often used to mitigate the harsh impact of the old slab system. By making an MDR claim, the purchaser would be able to compute their SDLT by reference to the average value of each property.

Lord Wilkinson owns the freeholds of four houses and because he wishes to move all his property into Wilkinson Limited they are linked transactions. We have to use market value as they are connected persons and these come in with two of the houses valued at £150,000 each and the other two at £300,000.

On a purchase price of £900,000 the SDLT due would be £62,000.

However the transactions involving the houses are relevant transactions for the purposes of the relief. The rate of tax on these transactions is set by the total consideration given in these transactions (£900,000) divided by the number of dwellings (4). This is £225,000. The SDLT due on £225,000 is £8,750 so multiplied by 4 gets us to £35,000 SDLT due. So by making this election Lord Wilkinson saves himself £27,000 SDLT.

For purchases of 6 or more residential properties in the same transaction, the purchaser will be able to choose whether multiple dwellings relief, with the higher 3% rates, will apply, or the non-residential rates (which will be charged on the total purchase price).

King Richard Hill purchases 10 additional residential properties in one transaction, for a total of £3 million. The average purchase price is therefore £300,000. He is purchasing 6 or more residential properties in the same transaction, so he can chose whether multiple dwellings relief, with the higher rates, will apply, or the non-residential rates.

Multiple dwellings relief:

The SDLT due, with the higher rates applied, on the average purchase price of £300,000 is £14,000. This is then multiplied by the number of properties (10) to give the total amount of SDLT due - £140,000.

Non-residential rates:

The non-residential rates apply to the total transaction value - £3 million. As this is in the 4% band, SDLT will be due at 4% on £3 million - £120,000. In this instance, King Hill will choose to pay under the non-residential rates and thus save himself £20,000 in SDLT

So where is this relevant? Say that you've met an investor who's fed up with the buy-to-let market and wants to get rid of his portfolio. Leaving aside the potential capital gains issues, you could take any number of properties off him and they would be averaged for SDLT.

More importantly, if you have a portfolio of property that you wish to put into a limited company, leaving aside the potential capital gains issues, they would be averaged for SDLT as per the examples above.

3.1.4   Fixtures and fittings

The removal of SDLT thresholds means that negotiating around various thresholds has become less important, but nonetheless there are still savings to be made with regard to fixtures & fittings.

It's important to understand that *fixtures* are part and parcel of the house that you are purchasing and will attract SDLT – so you can't avoid SDLT by agreeing with the vendor to pay via a separate contract for the kitchen, bathroom etc.

On the other hand, *moveable fittings* are not part of the fabric; as the name suggests, they are 'moveable'.

No SDLT will be payable for any items such as carpets, furniture, curtains and white goods, so if you like the current carpets, curtains and the huge American fridge that is too big for the removal company to shift, along with the 50" flatscreen TV, then it is possible and acceptable to agree that part of the agreed purchase price for these items and thus reduce SDLT. In the example above where we are buying a property for £275,000 if we could agree a price of say £25,000 for the fixtures and fittings that could potentially save £1,250 which could go towards legal or moving fees. The saving would be even greater if the 3% surcharge was applicable.

Now, I appreciate that with some of the stock you will be buying the last thing you want to do is hang on to the carpets – but if you can agree a price and it saves you SDLT it's worth a negotiation or two.

After all, it makes no difference to the vendor, who still receives the same price – simply as two tranches.

However you must be reasonable. As I alluded to earlier, HMRC naturally takes an interest in all transactions which are around SDLT thresholds. Remember that it is only moveable fittings that you are purchasing this way and, while there is no actual limit to what the vendor and buyer agree, it needs to be proportionate to the house – and capable of substantiation if HMRC requires it. HMRC's default position will be that you are trying to abuse the system – it will be up to you to persuade them otherwise!

3.2   Removal of the 10% Wear & Tear Allowance

The difference between 'rental income' and 'furnished rental income' is, spookily, the word 'furnished'!

So what is a furnished property?

Well, HMRC tells us:

"A furnished property is one that is capable of normal occupation without the tenant having to provide their own beds, chairs, tables, sofas and other furnishings, cooker etc. The provision of nominal furnishings will not meet this requirement."

Helpfully, though, they then fail to tell us what their definition of 'nominal furnishings' is, so in the absence of that insight I would suggest that – as long as they have somewhere to eat, somewhere to relax, somewhere to sleep and a reasonable carpet under their feet – then they have a furnished property. It may not be to your particular taste but, hey, this is a box to make us money.

No initial allowance will be given for the capital costs incurred when you furnish the property at the outset, but thereafter HMRC will allow a deduction for the fact that your property is furnished.

The deduction is given in one of two ways:

Replacement cost of goods – but not initial cost *or* a Wear and Tear Allow̤ which is currently 10% of the net rental income. So say your rentals were £10,00̤ before expenses then the deduction in your accounts would be £1,000. Let's say you paid the rates which amounted to £1,500 then your net rental amounts to £8,500 and thus the deduction would be only £850.

Sadly this 10% Wear and Tear Allowance is withdrawn from April 2016.

The original reason for implementing the 'Wear and Tear' allowance was to save landlords of furnished properties the bother of keeping detailed records. In its consultation paper HMRC state that *"they believe that the administration impact on landlords will be negligible",* (possibly because they don't live in the real world), *"as they are already required to keep records of other expenses"*. This belief does not take into account those landlords who own a number of fully furnished properties who up until now have not been required to keep detailed records.

The government have unfortunately spotted that the 10% was exceedingly generous. Wear and Tear Allowance is dependent on the amount of rental income received and this has the consequence that where rental income is higher the allowance is naturally much higher so that similar properties in different parts of the country will attract different levels of deductions despite having incurred similar levels of expenditure. Think rent to rent and HMO's and you will know how that the rent roll will be significant and thus deduction can be significant for little outlay.

HMRC estimate that this will produce additional revenue of £205 Million in 2016/17 which is why there's been much gnashing of teeth amongst landlords.

The new rules replace this generous Wear and Tear Allowance with a relief that enables all landlords to deduct the costs of replacing furnishings in the property. The initial cost of furnishing a property will, as before, not be included.

The new relief will cover the capital cost of replacing items provided for the tenant's use in the dwelling house, such as:

urniture or furnishings, such as beds or suites;

;

l freezers;

{ floor coverings;

...;

- linen;
- crockery or cutlery; and
- beds and other furniture.

Fixtures integral to the building, such as baths, fitted kitchen units and boilers that are not normally removed by the owner when the property is sold are not included. This is because the replacement cost of such items would, as now, be a deductible expense as a repair to the property itself.

The relief will apply from April 2016 to landlords of unfurnished, part furnished and furnished properties and whilst yet not enacted sure as night follows day we as landlords have to think about what we can do.

If you've been claiming the Wear and Tear Allowance you currently do not get any relief if you replace say a washing machine. So, from now on (April 2016), you can deduct the cost of replacement items where in the past you could not.

Note that HMRC don't want to see any betterment. So what does mean in practice? Well, if you provide a basic TV and it goes bang you can't replace with an Ultra HD TV and claim the full cost which is restricted to the original cost of the item. Harsh I know, however if you're providing high level furnished accommodation with state of the art TV system, then when you replace you can claim the new cost as you are replacing like with like.

Tenants may suffer in instances where the landlords' tax bill is higher on the withdrawal of the 10% allowance. Where margins are low some landlords might not be able to afford to replace or even supply furniture. Landlords may therefore be discouraged from making improvements if it leaves them out of pocket, the number of furnished properties may reduce, plus there's the chance rents will rise.

It will not apply to furnished holiday letting businesses and letting of commercial properties, because these businesses receive relief through the capital allowances regime. So it's business as usual there.

3.3   Rent-a-room Relief Increased up to £7,500

To generate some additional income you may choose to let out a room to a lodger in your home. If you do, then you can claim rent-a-room relief whereby you can earn £4,250 tax free. Yes, that's tax free.

Note that it must be your home and not a property that you are currently letting from a landlord.

You will provide the lodger with a furnished room and shared use of all common rooms and, maybe, make an additional charge for meals cleaning or laundry. So long as this is below £4,250, you have no tax to pay. That amount will apply up to 2015/16.

The even better news is that the tax free amount has now been increased to £7,500 from 6 April 2016, so you really have no excuse for filling that spare room with clutter when you could be turning it into an income generating stream. Yes there are some lifestyle changes to consider and you may have to invest in a dressing gown to visit the bathroom but £7,500 tax free!

Tax Tip

If, after deducting expenses, you have a loss then that loss can be offset against other rental income, assuming that you have some. The trick here is not to go the rent-a-room relief route but combine with all your property income on the tax return.

If the rental income exceeds £4,250 (2015/16), £7,500 (2016/17 onwards) then you will be taxed on rental income less expenses.

You now have the choice to take advantage of another tax tip.

3.4   Loan Interest and Finance Charges

Whilst there has been a technical update here I make no apologies for reminding you how important it is to claim the appropriate tax relief because this is an area where some may leave your money on the HMRC table. Notwithstanding the changes that will come in and how the relief will be applied, you would be amazed at the tax relief that can be obtained on your borrowings and interest. Interest is an allowable expense and whilst, on the face of it, you would think it fairly straightforward where interest would be claimed you may not be claiming for all that you can claim for.

Essentially loan interest is allowable on:

- Capital which has been introduced into the property business
- Other funds that have been used within the property business.

Let's look at each in turn.

Capital into the business

When a property first enters the letting market the value of that property at that time represents capital which has been introduced into the business. In addition, any other costs incurred in bringing that property to the market (such as stamp duty, legal fees, repairs, etc.) will be allowable, so any interest incurred in meeting those capital costs should be claimed against your profits.

Calder had a property in which he lived, with a great deal of equity; he only had a small mortgage of £50,000.

His house was worth £200,000, so he borrowed a further £100,000; this meant that he now had allowable borrowings of £150,000. The value of that property was £200,000 when it entered the lettings market and the amount of borrowings was £150,000.

He has two choices:

1. He could spend the £100,000 on buying more houses and clearly that would qualify for tax relief in its own right

2. If he so desired, he could cruise the world or buy a fast new car and still obtain tax relief on that additional debt.

In either situation he will obtain tax relief on the interest paid because the value of the new debt £100,000 was in situ when the property first entered the lettings market.

Tax Tip

Maximise the good debt on an asset before it enters the lettings market; if you have to use some of that good debt to clear the expensive bad debt of credit card liabilities.

A more traditional approach but nonetheless equally relevant is as follows:

O'Driscoll buys a house for £100,000 which he knows is well below market value. With a 75% buy-to-let mortgage he will obtain tax relief on his borrowings of £75,000.

All the usual work is undertaken to add value and after six months he looks to remortgage the property. The surveyor attends and, because he is having a good day, has not had a row with his other half and is feeling positive about life he values the property correctly at £130,000.

Pleased as punch, O'Driscoll then borrows 75% of the £130,000, getting full tax relief on the interest paid on borrowings of £97,500. Note that this is still below the capital value of the property when it entered the lettings market. After repaying the original mortgage, taking account of legal and borrowing fees, O'Driscoll is perfectly free to spend the extra cash released on what he wants. However, being a savvy property investor, he recycles the cash into another property.

Let's roll the clock forward, say ten years, and assume that the doom and gloom is behind us and that the property is now worth £200,000. O'Driscoll wants to release some of the equity in the property. Well 75% of £200,000 is £150,000 so what borrowings will qualify for tax relief?

Initially it will be 100/150ths: the 100 being the initial value when it entered the market and the 150 being the value of borrowings now. Yes, O'Driscoll can do what he likes with the money – but he will need to apportion the interest charge.

Or does he? If O'Driscoll uses those funds in the property business, maybe to provide working capital, pay for training or on-going running costs, then the money spent

here will enable the debt to qualify for tax relief. Equally, if as above, the funds are rolled over and used to provide money to put down as a deposit for a new investment property, then tax relief will be given on the interest.

> **Tax Tip**
>
> You will begin to see that you will need to keep careful records (spreadsheets usually work best) of where the cash released ultimately was spent; but there is no reason why careful record keeping will not prevent one of the biggest expenses, namely loan interest, being 100% tax deductible.

Other funds used in the business

Providing working capital to your business is where interest qualifies in the second category, but it need not be from remortgaged property.

These days nearly everybody makes a purchase on a credit card, so why not have one card used solely for your property business. In the event that you can't pay off the bill in full then the penal amount of interest that the credit card company charges is an allowable expense.

Back uses a dedicated credit card so that there can be no dispute that the interest charged is for the property business. If you stick in groceries and other personal living expenses then such interest will need to be apportioned and, while it can be done, that's time consuming and not a good use of your or your accountant's time.

> **Tax Tip**
>
> Use a dedicated credit card for business and if unable to clear the debt for whatever reason the interest will be tax deductible.

If you have managed to secure a bank overdraft, then congratulations are in order. They were what banks used to give to customers to help them grow their business, though to be fair some are now venturing back into the market. So if you have one, treasure and nurture it; all interest and costs associated with this will be allowable, even the charges applied and the punitive fixed fee they charge you simply to renew the overdraft.

More likely, in the absence of a sympathetic bank manager, you sourced a personal loan or joint venture finance; if the funds were used in your business, maybe to pay for training or to a builder, then please claim the interest paid.

Finance Charges

The final area that we need to look at under finance is loan arrangement fees and the impact of early redemption fees. Whilst there has never been any doubt that these are tax deductible, typically they were written off over the term of the loan if they were even written off at all. I still meet people who say that they've not written these costs off! Without getting too technical these can now be written off in full in the year they are incurred or to the extent that previously they were being written over the term of the loan in the current tax year.

Financial Reporting Standard for smaller entities (effective January 2015) states at 12.4:

Where an arrangement fee is such as to represent a significant additional cost of finance when compared with the interest payable over the life of the instrument, the treatment set out in paragraph 12.2 shall be followed. Where this is not the case it shall be charged in the profit and loss account immediately it is incurred.

For good measure here's para 12.2: *"The finance costs of borrowings shall be allocated to periods over the term of the borrowings at a constant rate on the carrying amount. All finance costs shall be charged in the profit and loss account."*

What that means to you, a property investor, is that any arrangement fee is not significant compared to the interest that you will be paying over the term of the loan and thus it's appropriate to write this off when incurred.

When completing the return, these will be finance charges and not interest costs and thus not affected by the new interest restriction rules. Make sure that you or your accountant put these costs in the correct box on the tax return to avoid any restrictions in the tax relief obtained.

I'm often asked about early repayment charges when we switch loans and I would always say that they are allowable in full as the change in borrowing was a commercial decision. You wanted to move to a better interest rate, release capital to go investing again, though strangely HMRC may treat these as personal costs.

> **Tax Tip**
>
> As I've said elsewhere if you document why you switched and can clearly demonstrate that it was a business decision then continue to claim early repayment charges on your tax return.

3.5   Principal Private Residence Exemption (PPR)

I'm sure that all of you know, but it does no harm to remind you that you can avoid some CGT on a property if it has, at some stage, been classed as your only or main residence.

Indeed, if the property was your only or main residence throughout the period of ownership then the profit made on the sale of your main home – no matter how large the gain – is completely exempt from CGT and is covered by the PPR exemption. Nothing ground breaking there!

However, used correctly and combined with other reliefs – and the fact that, for some of this period, the property doesn't even have to be your main home – it is possible to generate significant gains; and, yes, they will be tax-free! Every unmarried individual and legally married couple is entitled to the principal private residence exemption for their only or main residence – and, even better, the PPR extends to cover the last eighteen months (previously three years of) ownership.

Uttley bought a house in 2005. He lived in it and then moved out in March 2015. He did not sell it until March 2016 – the entire period of ownership and gain would be exempt and covered by the PPR.

There is no reason why this property could not be let out for up to eighteen months (and being a good responsible taxpayer Uttley would include the rental income, less all relevant costs on his self-assessment return) because the PPR always extends to this last period of ownership. There is, of course, no need to sell the property after the eighteen months whilst you will no longer qualify for PPR there is, luckily, another relief coming your way in the form of Letting Relief that will assist with a tax free disposal.

Tax Tip

To be fully exempt from Capital Gains Tax and make use of the PPR it's important that it became your only or main residence immediately on purchase, or it was your only or main residence at some point and you sold it no more than eighteen months after purchase. If you can't tick either box then you will still get a proportion of the relief plus your last eighteen months.

Chapter 4

Buy to Let Income Changes

As alluded to earlier this is the biggest shake up in the BTL market and needless to say the changes are not without its critics. For me as an investor it seems fundamentally wrong that interest costs in purchasing an asset (in this case a house) to make money should be restricted in this case to a 20% deduction. No other business in the UK has such draconian restrictions. If Manchester United, there are other Premier League clubs around, borrow money to buy a player, and yes they will be an asset, there is no restriction on the tax relief they obtain, so why go after the landlord?

The bigger picture seems to be that the government does not like the boom in the buy-to-let market. In particular, the Chancellor dislikes the fact that savvy individuals (people like you and me) are taking advantage of low interest rates to hoover up properties that he would rather see acquired by owner-occupiers. The clamour from some, particularly Ian Cowie at The Sunday Times, that it is "not fair" that landlords obtain tax relief for interest, but owner-occupiers do not, seems to have finally been listened to no matter how unjust! Investors have to find a 25% deposit and homeowners do not, so there is nothing to stop homebuyers making good use of the lower interest rates, Plus investors pay CGT if they sell a property while those selling their main home do so free of any tax! That doesn't look a very level playing field to me!

According to a survey from lettings agents Your Move and Reeds Rains, many fear letting out a property will become far less profitable when the reforms start to come into force in April 2017 and they are now considering leaving the sector as a result! This loss of enthusiasm is even dampening the optimism of the 31% of landlords who think that now is a good time to buy rental properties and 44% believe investing in buy to let property is more complicated than it was six months ago.

Clause 24 limits tax relief to the basic rate for interest on loans taken to acquire buy-to-let property.

This is a fundamental change and I continue to be surprised at the number of investors who do not fully understand the impact of this change and how it will impact on portfolio profitability.

Even more worrying there are accountants out there who don't understand it and thus are unable to proactively advise their clients!

The new rules operate by requiring, in the first instance, that profits are computed without regard to the relevant interest payments. There is then a separate relief – a "tax reduction". This is calculated by reference to basic rate tax on an amount equal to the interest payments.

The changes are phased in over three years starting from 6 April 2017, with the new rules applying to 25% of the relevant interest in the first year, 50% in the second and 75% in the third. They bite in full on all relevant interest payments from 6 April 2020.

Although their impact is softened by the delayed and phased introduction, the changes will affect the economics of some buy-to-let portfolios significantly. So start looking now at how this will impact on you.

The effect of the new rules is merely to restrict tax relief to the basic rate of tax, so some of you may think that you will not be affected. I'm afraid I've some bad news as this simple example demonstrates.

Thomas has a modest salary of £35,000 which is supplemented with a BTL property generating net income of £8,000 (Gross rent of £14,000 less interest costs of £4,000 and other costs of £2,000). So his total income is £43,000 which after deducting a personal allowance of £11,000 leaves a taxable income of £32,000 which is all taxed at the basic rate.

Under the new rules when fully applied Thomas' salary will be added to his rental income before interest is deducted so his taxable income is now £47,000 (Gross rent of £14,000 less other costs of £2,000 plus salary of £35,000) which means that £4,000 of income is taxed at 40% From this is deducted the interest charge which will be £4,000 at 20% (£800), so his overall tax bill has risen by £800 simply through this rule change.

Thomas is not untypical of one of those people I mentioned earlier, over 55 who've taken a chunk of cash from their pension pot and bought a BTL property. How can that be just and equitable?

That was with one property: imagine the impact if he had a portfolio of say 6 or even much bigger? There are some real horror stories about people who've built a portfolio, who yes are highly geared (level of debt to equity) who now face all profits being wiped out by these changes. So they are the one in five referred to who need to take action sooner rather than later.

This is where I think that The Chancellor and his friend the Governor of the Bank of England have not thought this through. We are told that Clause 24 is designed, along with other measures, to dampen down the demand in the BTL sector. In certain cases this will make landlords unprofitable and they may decide to dump portfolios on the market. Now we have a surplus of supply and in drastic cases landlords may simply hand the keys back to the banks: a return to the last property crash. Is this really what he wants to achieve?

The new restrictions apply to the costs of a "dwelling-related loan". This means any amount borrowed for the purpose of a property business carried on to generate income from dwelling houses.

However it does not apply to a business of dealing in property or developing property for sale, only to property letting ones. So those of you flipping property in your own name you are OK, though as a general rule I would flip through a limited company.

Even worse though, this restriction does not just apply to loans taken out specifically to acquire properties for letting. In principle, the restriction also applies to a loan taken out to acquire a motor vehicle used in the management of a property business, or office accommodation from which a property business is run.

The main effect, though, will be on loans taken out to acquire property for letting.

The restriction is very specific in its application. First, it applies only to the letting of dwelling houses with an appropriate apportionment where a loan relates in part to a business of letting residential property and in part to some other business, say letting commercial property. So, say you had a mixed portfolio the restrictions at present would only apply to the residential side. So it might be that you structure your debt in favour of the commercial units: by increasing the debt on these units and paying off residential BTL debt you will lessen the impact of the interest tax relief changes.

The new rules are expressed not to apply to a property business "carried on by a company": methinks George wants us all to run off and form limited companies as they are much easier to keep track of! There were some rumblings about property companies, but so far they all seem to have come to nothing, though never rule out the moves of a Chancellor determined to rein in the BTL sector.

The new rules do, however, apply to individuals, partnerships and limited liability partnerships. A strict reading of the legislation would suggest that a property business carried on by a partnership with even a single corporate member would be outside the new rules because such a business is undoubtedly "carried on by a company".

I suggest that maybe they haven't thought of some of the creative structures used by us investors, so I guess expect a more keen interest from HMRC and a strategy that may be governed by your risk profile.

There is some good news in that the restrictions do not apply to a loan which is "referable to so much of a property business as consists of the commercial letting of furnished holiday accommodation". So maybe that's something to consider through changes to your portfolio.

4.1   Incorporation

The million $ question is always should I use a limited company. And the Million $ answer is "it depends"! That's not to be evasive, but there are so many factors to consider and we will look at some of these below.

Operating a business through a company has always had the attraction that profits are taxed at company rates of tax. The fact that the new interest rules do not apply to companies may further increase the attraction of operating a residential property lettings business through a company. But there will be all kinds of costs to consider.

Some things to consider about incorporation:

Firstly, if all profits are being extracted, in other words all profits go to fund your lifestyle then the introduction of the new rates of dividend tax from April 2016 (see chapter 6) will likely result in the aggregate tax payable on profits routed through a company probably exceeding the tax payable on profits earned by an individual directly. In some cases this additional tax alone will outweigh any savings from maintaining full tax relief on interest. So don't rush to incorporate!

Second, there is the potential double charge to taxation for a capital gain made in a company where if once sold you want to get your hands on the money!
Duckham, a property investor made a net property gain of £100,000, and leaving aside annual allowances would create a tax bill of £28,000 if made personally, leaving £72,000 net. If that same gain were made in a company Duckham Limited, the corporation tax would be £20,000 and further tax on distribution if that money were then to be paid as a dividend (i.e. putting the money in his pocket to spend) of around £26,000, leaving only £54,000 net.

Then again do you plan to hold in perpetuity or maybe sell off later in life?

Third what about death? It happens to us all and property ownership, be it personal or corporate is treated differently on death. When properties are owned directly, Inheritance Tax will be calculated by reference to their values at the date of death (net of debt) but, importantly, the properties will be "re-based" to market value for Capital Gains Tax purposes. So, if the Executors or even the beneficiaries then sell there will therefore not normally be any capital gains tax charge if sold soon after probate. If held for longer then the value at probate will be your base cost for any subsequent capital gain.

Edwards owned a row of cottages valued at £500,000 with debt of £200,000 so ignoring all other allowances and assets on his demise Inheritance Tax of £120,000 will be due. His son Edwards Junior would be deemed to have acquired the properties at £500,000, which he could then sell and the 500,000 proceeds would be free from capital gains tax.

Without being flippant, a good way to avoid CGT is to die because the assets are rebased going forward. However CGT bites at potentially 28% and IHT at 40%, though as can be seen in the above example debt reduces the impact of IHT. It would not be considered when assessing CGT, so if Edwards had sold his portfolio and say he acquired them many years ago for £100,000, the CGT liability would be £112,000. This demonstrates nicely that there is always a pay off between CGT and IHT. Compare that to shares in a property-owning company. Inheritance Tax will be due by reference to the value of the shares at the date of death, and they will be "re-based" to market value for Inheritance Tax purposes. In other words the value of the share for probate will be based on the market values of the property. But there will be no "re-basing" of the properties themselves. In other words the properties stay in the company with massive capital gains locked in.

This may be less of a concern if the property company passes to beneficiaries and continues to be run without substantial changes, but it may add significantly to the tax costs if, on death, the portfolio is sold and the proceeds distributed between beneficiaries. That said there are some great planning opportunities within a company structure and we will look at these later.

For those with an existing portfolio, the costs (including tax costs) of transferring the properties to a company will need to be considered. If the properties have increased in value then Capital Gains Tax will be an issue. It may be possible to show that the activity amounts to a "business" such that incorporation relief may be available. If that is the case, the opportunity for a "tax-free" rebasing of the properties is an additional attraction. We will look at these considerations in greater detail in the next chapter.

In every case Stamp Duty Land Tax will also need to be considered and this may prevent a straight transfer into a limited company. However where there's an existing partnership or limited liability partnership FA 2003, Sch 15 (sorry it's technical but that's what it's called) may offer opportunities for relief from SDLT. The rules are complex and as they likely to cause most people to doze off I will spare you a full and detailed synopsis. Suffice to say husband and wife with a large portfolio, dedicated bank account, partnership tax returns filed along with individual self-assessment returns and run as a bona fide business have far more chance of tax relief here. So speak to your trusted solicitor to see if you will qualify for this relief.

Chapter 5

How to Deal with Those Changes

The changes to relief for interest costs related to buy-to-let properties are likely to have a profound effect on the economics of many residential property portfolios. So start planning now! As I've said before you've four years before the new rules bite in full, so take action to minimise the impact.

Look at all your options. What's the rental income likely to be, what are the expected costs that can be deducted and what will be the interest deduction? I think you also need to consider the costs of any changes to the way your portfolio is structured and yes there may well be one off pain. So see what that pain is and is it a cost that long term will provide you with a better and more tax efficient portfolio?

Daft as it may seem, but where do you see yourself and your portfolio in five or even ten years' time? Big picture planning, the stuff we help our valued clients with is so important and whilst you may not have got the structure right initially or George has forced you to reconsider there's never been a better time to start.

The key thing is not to panic!

So what could you do faced with this change to interest relief?

Here's a few which we'll flesh out below:

1. May not impact
2. Incorporate
3. Load expenses
4. Changes to portfolio
5. Income splitting
6. Put rent up!
7. Sell!

So let's look at each in turn mindful of the fact that there is no magic wand and you will need to consider how the changes impact on you and then take action.

1.   May not impact

David Gauke, financial secretary to the Treasury at the sitting of the Public Bill Committee advised that only one in five landlords is expected to pay more tax as a result of the changes.

It may be that you derive all your income from property and have very little debt. In which case you can earn £43,000 (personal allowance of £11,000 plus 20% basic rate band) in income before higher rates taxes come into force. With properties held jointly that's an income of £84,000. For those of you with little or no debt then the interest reliefs will have little impact, but before you get too smug have you thought about the impact of Inheritance Tax on the portfolio that you've built up?

It may be that you could sell a property (yes there may be capital gains and we'll cover that later) but the cash released could then be used to clear down debt on some of your other properties, mindful of course of any Early Repayment Charges. OK you've one less income generating property, but overall your portfolio may be more tax efficient.

It may be that you've significant losses from previous property projects such that at the present time there's no need to rush to incorporate.

Review your portfolio to see if there are some mortgages that could be moved to a more favourable rate, which in turn will reduce the impact of the restriction because the interest charge will be less. Yes the lending criteria are becoming more stringent with lenders wanting more information on your personal expenditure, but there are still some great rates out there. Some of you may still have loans on crazy interest rates of base plus 1%, so it would make commercial sense not to move away from those, but invest some time to look at your portfolio and see if you could restructure your borrowings.

Is there a property in your portfolio that is not generating the income and thus is a liability not an asset? Now may be a good time to offload and use the cash generated either to clear debt or put towards more income generating assets.

2.   Incorporate

Many property forums are awash with comment about incorporation and it's good that the debate is out there, but moving your properties into a limited company is not a global panacea and is not right for everybody. Diagnosis without prognosis is malpractice, so beware of taking advice on forums or benefitting from what I call "gin and tonic tax advice". There are thousands of people out there who prefer to do their own self assessment returns and I have no issue with that at all, but be careful of what you don't know and whilst I would say this wouldn't I, with all the changes going on now might be a good time to burn some money for professional advice. There is no one magic answer as all of us are at different stages on our property journey.

Whilst if you were a higher rate taxpayer I would always have advised using a company, and it still amazes me how many higher rate tax payers bought in their own names, until recently one of the biggest challenges was the availability of good old fashioned BTL finance to newly formed companies. That I'm pleased to say is behind us with banks who now lend at rates not dissimilar to a simple BTL mortgage. Indeed banks are having to offer BTL products or they will lose market share. For all the grief that the Governor of the Bank of England gives BTL investors, banks are gradually realising that there are people out there buying property who in turn will make money for the bank! Yes, they are more cautious and the days of NINJA (no income no job no assets) mortgages are well behind us. Thankfully same day mortgages as well, so investors now go after yield not capital growth which in turn means the ability to pay interest only mortgages provides greater cover for lenders.

For me there are three hurdles to consider when looking at incorporation:

a)   Potential Capital Gains Tax
b)   Potential SDLT issues
c)   Funding issues

a) Potential Capital Gains Tax

If you are the owner of a property and you sell to a company which is controlled by you then you are a connected person and thus the sale has to be at market value. As smart investors who've bought below market value I'd like to think that you are sitting on capital gains.

One off disposals

At present 2016/17 the first £11,100 of any capital gain is tax free so potentially a gain of £22,200 on one property held jointly by a married couple could see the property move into a new company with no capital gains tax to pay. So in theory if you have, say a few properties between 2016/17 and 2019/20 when the restrictions bite in full you could transfer a property each year and make use of the annual exemption.

Mr & Mrs Dawes are sitting on a portfolio of four houses sitting on capital gains of between £15,000 and £20,000. Ignoring for the moment SDLT and CGT and borrowings, they could transfer a property to Dawes Limited (one a year 2016/17 through to 2019/20) and as long as the gain was less than £22,200 no CGT would be due.

You may have properties that are not held in joint names, so now might be a good time to get your partner on the deeds to make use of their annual exemption should you decide to incorporate. Note that there's a potential SDLT issue here if you take over debt and you will need to speak to your mortgage company. As always weigh up the costs and benefits and see if doing this will work for you.

You may have within your portfolio a property that was initially your main residence or indeed two. So whilst on the face of it the capital gains may be excessive it could be that with Principal Residence Relief, the last 18 months along with letting relief means that the actual taxable capital gain is quite small.

Such a simple explanation is worthy of an example.

Morris bought a house in April 2005 for £126,000. He lived in the property for four years and then moved away for work and chose to let out the property for a further seven years, when he sold the property for £225,000 in April 2016. In all, he owned the property for eleven years. Ignoring legal and selling costs, for the purpose of this example he is sitting on a gain of £99,000.

Firstly we calculate his PPR. He has owned it and lived in it for four years and can also claim the last eighteen months so his PPR will be 5.5/11 of £99,000 £49,500 leaving £49,500 taxable.

As £40,000 is below £49,500 (the actual gain before letting relief) Morris can deduct a further £40,000 from his calculations.

So now the taxable gain is £9,500 (£99,000 - £49,500 - £40,000). As that amount is below the Annual Exemption there will be no tax Capital Gains Tax to pay. If he'd bought the property as an investment – his tax bill would have been £27,720 (28% of £99,000).

So whilst on the face of it there was a large capital gain, Morris could sell to a third party or sell to his newly formed company and pay no CGT.

Tax Tip

If the property is bought in joint names, then the husband and wife or registered civil partner can each claim the private letting relief. So the smarter ones amongst you will appreciate that that represents £80,000 worth of gain on which you can avoid CGT!

Tax Tip

The private letting relief calculation needs to be made for every property which has been your only or main residence at any time during its ownership. So, if desired or needed, you could sell two (or even more) homes that you have at some stage lived in, and collect the letting relief of £40,000.

Even better if you have followed the tax tip above then that's £80,000 per property on which you can avoid CGT. Happy days!

Larger Portfolios

If you have a larger portfolio then you could look at obtaining Incorporation Tax Relief. In a nutshell there would be no gain on the sale of the portfolio to a limited company and the gain would be held over. Incorporation Relief is given if the business, together with the whole of its assets (or all its assets other than cash) is transferred, the business is transferred as a going concern, and the business is transferred in exchange wholly or partly for shares in the transferee company.

The relief is given automatically and there is no need to make a claim. The relief works by reducing the base cost of the new assets by a proportion of the gain arising from the disposal of the old assets. So we take a portfolio of property and sell to ABC Ltd in exchange for shares in that company. The properties go into the company at current cost and the shares if sold have a lower value for CGT when sold.

Some are seeing this as a get out of jail card for incorporation and avoiding CGT, but a word of caution. It's no global panacea and not a case of one size fits all.

Historically, HMRC's view was incorporation tax relief could not apply to property investments. This view was successfully challenged at the Upper Tribunal in *Ramsay v HMRC*.

Mrs Ramsay owned a block of 15 flats. She had inherited a one-third share, but later acquired the other two thirds from her brothers with a bank loan. The property was later transferred to a company. She applied for planning permission to refurbish and redevelop the property, although no work had been done at the time of the transfer. The Ramsay's dealt with the management and maintenance of the property themselves, spending around 20 hours per week on it, and had no other occupation during the period.

Without getting too technical the Upper Tribunal decided that the correct approach was to 'consider whether Mrs Ramsay's activities were a 'serious undertaking earnestly pursued' or a 'serious occupation'; whether they were an occupation or function pursued with reasonable or recognisable continuity; whether they had substance in terms of turnover; whether they were conducted in a regular manner and on sound recognised business principles; and whether they were of a kind that are commonly made by those who seek to profit by them. It concluded they were.
The First Tier Tribunal had previously decided in favour of HMRC. The Upper Tribunal said the First Tier Tribunal's approach was incorrect, because they had focused on the meaning of trade rather than business.

HMRC's *Capital Gains Manual* (it's CG65715 if you can't sleep) now states: 'The *Ramsay* case .... confirming that for there to be a business for incorporation relief there has to be "activity" and that just a modest degree of activity would not suffice. It also shows us that it is the quantity not the quality of the activity that is important.'

For me Ramsey and the HMRC guidance leave some uncertainty. What degree of activity is required by the taxpayer? If the Ramsays had not applied for planning permission for redevelopment, would their activity still have constituted a business? If the Ramsays had used a managing agent, would it still have constituted a business? As with a trade, it should not matter whether the taxpayer uses an agent, but this isn't certain from the case, or HMRC's guidance.

As a general rule I'd like to see at least ten properties, so that it's possible to put a case together, though I accept that one person may have three properties that keeps them occupied full time.

I predict a rush to claim this relief and as it's self-policing through self-assessment I believe that HMRC will look for a weak case and then seek to get the judgement in Ramsey replaced by more recent case law which is clearly in their favour.

Where the gains on the portfolio are large, it would be advisable to seek an HMRC non-statutory clearance. By that you stick your head over the parapet and tell HMRC what you are proposing. You can ask HMRC for further guidance or advice if you:

- have fully considered the relevant guidance and/or contacted the relevant helpline
- have not been able to find the information you need
- remain uncertain about HMRC's interpretation of tax legislation

HMRC will then set out their advice in writing and you can then proceed with incorporation. If there is some doubt I would recommend going this route rather than adopt the "hit and hope" approach. If challenged by HMRC the tax bill could be substantial and they could look for interest and penalties.

Clearly with two BTL properties and a full time job you would struggle, but the bigger the portfolio and the size of the gain the more serious the consideration of pursuing this route.

You could also mix the two by a) folding properties into the limited company and b) also selling some over a period of time to make use of the annual Capital Gains Tax exemption or where the capital gains are covered by other reliefs as indicated above.

b)   Potential SDLT issues

If Mr & Mrs Jones form a company to transfer their properties they will clearly be connected with the company, thus the market value will always apply for SDLT. In Chapter 3 we looked at the changes to SDLT so here's a brief reminder of things to be aware of.

If you've a large portfolio this could be considerable though I would refer you to Chapter 3 and how averaging may apply if more than six properties or indeed the rules if less than six and you want to incorporate.

There is some good news here in that where the transferor is a partnership, this normal rule is overridden. The impact of these provisions can be that to the extent the company is connected with the partners making the transfer, which clearly they would be, no SDLT may arise.

Sounds too good to be true doesn't it, so just as with the Ramsey case proceed with caution before cracking out the champers because you've dodged the SDLT bullet!

HMRC's view is that mere joint ownership of property does not constitute a partnership! Take it from me, but if you can't sleep go here (HMRC's *Property Income Manual* at PIM1030), therefore it shouldn't be assumed that the properties held under partnership agreements can be transferred free of SDLT. For a partnership to exist there must be a business carried on in common with a view to profit. This is a general law issue, but it might follow similar principles to whether a business exists for *Ramsay* or capital gains purposes.

So as ever seek professional advice. As mentioned before, a husband and wife with a large portfolio, dedicated bank account, partnership tax returns filed along with individual self-assessment returns and run as a bona fide business have far more chance than two unrelated parties who own property together.

c) Funding Issues

Whatever size the portfolio it's likely that it's been built up leveraging other people's money (mainly banks) and have a portfolio with a managed amount of debt, but most likely scattered over a number of lenders and at various interest rates. You may still have some that are actually at base rate!

When you move your property into a new company chances are that you will have to consolidate the debt because at present the house will be secured in your names with the lender and you want to move the properties to ABC Ltd. Depending on who your lender is that could be quite easy or you may have to start afresh with a new bank. The fact that you are an established landlord and have been running a profitable portfolio will all be in your favour.

Either way finance is no longer the obstacle that it used to be. Sure the security will be the same (the property) but things to consider will be:

- What's the new interest rate
- Will I suffer any early repayment charges with my current mortgage
- Is my current mortgage so good I may as well stay where I am (effectively grin and bear it)

So, as well as CGT and SDLT it's spreadsheet time to see what the mortgage payments will be, what the rent will do and what will the ERC's be and then take a decision.

Only you will know if it's right or wrong but once made stick with the plan and see it through to the end. You weighed up the options and now it's time to take action and implement.

3.   Load expenses

As I continue to say, incorporation is not right for everyone and there's a school of thought that you buy in own names and build a portfolio which you remortgage every ten years to strip out tax free cash. Yes that works providing your rent roll finances the mortgage repayments and of course you will no longer get as much tax relief on the borrowings, so your tax bill will go up! Plus you recognise that long term your portfolio is exposed to Inheritance Tax.

Some may have a small portfolio, too small to benefit from other reliefs, that is sitting on massive capital gains and thus the pain in SDLT and CGT would be too great a one off cost to merit incorporation. Remember that we have to look at the impact of one off costs against future potential long term gains.

So you need to be being more streetwise with your expenditure. Many landlords choose to manage their own portfolios and also deal with all the maintenance issues. That's their choice, though one I prefer to avoid. But here's the thing, by doing the work themselves they are effectively doing the work for free because there is no deduction in your letting accounts for your "own time". You are effectively an unpaid rent collector or maintenance person.

If you are one of these people working for free then depending on the size of your portfolio it might be worth forming your own property management company to do this work and then charge this back as an expense to you as the landlord. If you think of all the steps in sorting a tenant, referencing, check in, EPC, maintenance jobs, not forgetting commission on collecting the rents, these all have a cost and with some of the larger agents these can be considerable.

The tenancy agreement is still between you and the tenant, but ABC Ltd stands between you both and the fees charged are a deduction in your letting accounts.

There needs to be a reasonable portfolio to make it work, but I've known clients do it with two or three properties.

Let's look at how this would work in practice. Remember Thomas from earlier?, he you will recall will be £800 a year worse off under the new rules.

Thomas has a modest salary of £35,000 which is supplemented with a BTL property generating net income of £8,000 (Gross rent of £14,000 less interest costs of £4,000 and other costs of £2,000. So his total income is £43,000 which after deducting a personal allowance of £11,000 leaves a taxable income of £32,000 which is all taxed at the basic rate.

Under the new rules when fully applied his salary will be added to his rental income before interest is deducted so his taxable income is now £47,000 which means that £4,000 of income is taxed at 40%. From this is deducted the interest charge which will be £4,000 at 20% (£800) so his overall tax bill has risen by £800 simply through this rule change.

Let's suppose his brother Thomas 2 also owns property but actually has three in his portfolio. I've kept the rents the same for ease of reference.

Thomas 2 has a modest salary of £35,000 which is supplemented with 3 BTL properties generating net income of £24,000 (Gross rent of £42,000 less interest costs of £12,000 and other costs of £6,000. So his total income is £59,000, which after deducting a personal allowance of £11,000 leaves a taxable income of £48,000 which is taxed (£32,000 at basic rate and £12,000 at 40%) giving a tax bill of £12,800.

If he put in place a management company and charged a modest 12.5% excluding any maintenance work he would be £1,050 better off in terms of income tax.

Yes there are formation costs in year one and ongoing compliance work, but tax savings to be made nonetheless.

But it's not just using a property management company: it's as I say being streetwise with expenditure to make sure that you claim for every cost in running your property business. So please keep a detailed record of all costs incurred from the simple postage stamp through to major costs like replacement boilers, roofs etc. All these costs will reduce the amount on which you pay tax. To butcher that annoying advert think where there's a cost there's a claim.

4.   Changes to portfolio

We discussed above how we could look at loading expenses to reduce the profit exposed to tax and thus the impact of these changes.

A portfolio change to furnished lettings where the interest rate deduction will not be restricted would certainly work. Done well the yields on holiday lets can be very rewarding. Yes they are harder work and the properties may not be in your location, but if the yield is better you may find them to be more rewarding than single lets. Some investors are now getting into serviced apartments along the Airbnb route, which again brings good yield, albeit you have to work harder for the income.

But you may just change the type of stock that you are buying. Moving away from the fluffy stuff that just needs a deep clean and is ready to go may bring rewards in other areas. Viewing stock that most investors shy away from is where there's gold a) in terms of adding value and b) the deductions that you can claim in year one to offset against all the profits from other properties.

Yes we're talking repairs and renewals here and as you know having purchased my Amazon best seller www.iainwallis.com/booksale done correctly the deductions are not to be sniffed at.

So add a couple of these to your portfolio, rinse and repeat and enjoy the benefits.

5.   Income splitting

For whatever reason you may have a portfolio where one partner holds 100% of the equity or even properties owned 50/50 where one of the parties does not work.

Let's look at property in a married couple where only one party is on the deeds. Well, if you are both 40% taxpayers then there's really very little that can be done here and it's back to the incorporation route.

However it may be that one partner is earning less, maybe even nothing at all. In that case we could look at transferring a share of the equity to the partner who is paying tax at a lower rate. Care needs to be taken as you will need to speak to the mortgage company and whilst there is no CGT issue on transfers between husband and wife, SDLT may be relevant as taking over 50% of the mortgage would be a consideration of value and thus SDLT is due. Again, it may be a small cost compared to the long term tax savings.

Once the property is in joint names then bash off Form P17 to HMRC to advise that rental income will now be taxed 80/20 or whatever you have worked out is the most tax efficient.

You may already own the property jointly and within the married unit one of the partners does not work or has a lower level of income. Instead of splitting the income 50/50 as above bash off a Form P70 to advise HMRC that the income will be split 90/10 in favour of the partner with lower income levels.

6. Put rent up!

Whilst George and the Governor of the Bank of England seem to think that landlords are the scourge of the earth because they have all the property stock (they don't, but it gets votes and makes good copy) they need to realise that the proposed measures may even worsen the availability of stock to the rental market.

A survey from lettings agents Your Move and Reeds Rains in November 2015 confirms that the current trend of tenant demand outstripping the supply of rental properties looks set to continue.
Some 52% of landlords have seen an increase in tenant demand during the past six months, up from 41% this time last year. And 34% also believe that if their current tenant chose to leave, they could find new occupants within their notice period.

Demand for homes to let is expected to exceed supply even more sharply in future. Over the next six months, 58% of landlords predict tenant demand will increase further. But only 22% of landlords are planning to grow their portfolio in the next year, putting the already limited supply of rental accommodation under more pressure. Some 35% say the main reason they will raise their rents next year is due to strong tenant demand for each available property.

As demand exceeds supply even those who aren't blessed with GCSE Economics will know that the price will rise. So if the market will take it, put the rent up. As always with rent reviews there's a fine line between upping the rent and then being hit with a barrage of little issues that the tenant was prepared to live with, plus the element of poker where the upheaval is so great the tenant will stay compared to the landlord not wanting voids.

It's always "take a view" and if the agents support it you can always say it's not my fault that there's a chronic shortage of housing here in the UK, plus if I can't make money then I'll sell and you'll have to find somewhere else to live. Yes I know we all want to be kind, considerate, caring landlords and not Rackman, but if your property is taking money out of your pocket and not putting it in, Robert Kiyosaki from his great book Rich Dad Poor Dad, will tell you that you've a liability not an asset.

7.   Sell!

Yes it's an option and possibly one that George wants you to follow and thus free up housing stock. Something tells me this might be who George is after, maybe the accidental landlord or someone just splitting their investment cash over a number of opportunities. All well and good, but George seems to have overlooked the fact that there are a lot of investors out there who will be only too willing to take stock off investors who no longer want to play monopoly for real. And guess what, even though they have to find 25% deposits they can move mighty fast, plus they don't have Mum and Dad pointing out why you don't want to buy a house in such and such an area.
All things considered though, it may be that you want out.

Selling any property may create a liability to Capital Gains Tax which at its simplest will be net proceeds minus gross costs, less your annual exemption for capital gains tax which is currently £11,000.

The mechanics of this are all within my original book so I won't repeat them here, but just give you a couple of ways to minimise the exit pain.

If you've held property for a long time then you could be sitting on quiet a large capital gain and potentially would lose up to 28% in CGT, though don't forget that there are some great reliefs available as listed above when we looked at CGT

If you do decide to sell then timing is everything. A sale pre 5 April 2017, to the extent there is tax to pay, will be due 31 January 2018. If you sell any time after then the capital gain will fall into the tax year 2017/18 in which case the tax will not be due until 31 January 2019, so time to squirrel the money away.

Here are two possible solutions that may reduce any potential Capital Gains Tax:

Furnished Holiday Lets

How about a change of direction and make the property a furnished holiday let? What this means is that it will qualify for the same CGT breaks as a business and for certain reliefs you only have to hold this property for a year.

Now some of you may be thinking hang on Iain my property's nowhere near the sea and a ready supply of fish and chip shops, nor is it nestled in Chipping Oddbury or some other sleepy picture postcard village. But here's the thing, it doesn't have to be!

To hit the brief as a furnished holiday let it must be:

a)   available for lets at least 210 days a year
b)   actually let for 105 of those
c)   not let for long periods (over 31) for than 155 days

Now some of my stock on the edge of The Bronx may not be suitable, but there are properties in major cities where people do visit either on business or holidays. We actually had someone stay in our holiday cottage for two weeks as it was cheaper and dare I say more relaxing than staying in a hotel.

As a genuine Furnished Holiday let you can claim Rollover Relief, which is not when you tell your partner to rollover as they are snoring, but where any gain made on the sale can be rolled over (deferred) into a replacement property. Even better the sale may attract Entrepreneurs' Relief which would reduce the CGT rate to 10%.

Let's have an example:

Adams is a higher rate taxpayer and has just sold a property that he bought four years ago and which for the last year he has let as a holiday home. The gain is £100,000 which on the face of it excluding the annual exemption is a tax bill of £28,000. As he intends to buy another property he can defer £5,600 (20% of the gain one of the five years at 28%).

Adams then claims Entrepreneurs' Relief and so 10% is applied to the gain after the rollover relief above, which will produce a tax bill of £8,000 (£100,000 gain less £20,000 rolled over at 10%). So a tax bill and deferred bill of £13,600 instead of £28,000.

It could be that a move into furnished holiday lets and thus still obtaining tax relief at your highest rate of tax is a way to go.

Make use of an Enterprise Investment Scheme (EIS)
By reinvesting sale proceeds from property sales you can shelter all of the gains on your property.

*Pullen sells a property for £250,000 that he bought for £150,000 twenty years ago. Ignoring any other reliefs Pullen has a tax bill of £28,000 (28% * £100,000). That CGT can be deferred indefinitely by investing £100,000 into one or more EIS companies with the gain only becoming taxable when he sells the EIS investment.*

Investing in EIS also qualifies you for tax relief equal to 30% of the investment £33.333. So from sale proceeds of £250,000 the amount that hits the bank account will be £183,333 (£250,000 - £100,000 + £33,333) and he has an EIS investment of £100,000. I'll leave out the debate about investing in EIS but as ever there's a payoff between risk and reward.

Both of these will reduce the pain on exiting the property market.

Chapter 6

Dividend Changes

Welcome to another Osborne stealth tax.

What's changed?

Up to 5 April 2016 dividends, the distribution of post corporation tax profits to company owners, were paid with a notional tax credit of 10% attached. What that meant was that with a nominal salary and dividends nearly £40,000 could be taken out of the company with no higher rate tax to pay and because the dividend came tax paid there was no further tax to pay. So yes, you needed to make the profits, but a husband and wife company could extract £80,000 effectively tax free. Happy days indeed.

We are now going to see the introduction of a new £5,000 dividend exemption, which everyone is entitled to, including those paying higher rate tax. Thereafter dividends for basic rate taxpayers will then be taxed at 7.5%, at 32.5% if paying tax at 40% and a new 38.1% for those paying the top rate of tax of 45%.

There was much initial confusion as to what the actual £5,000 represented, but HMRC have now provided some guidance. Essentially the £5,000 allowance will not be the extra tax exemption that people were hoping for, instead it is treated as a zero rate band only for dividend income. This results in the first £5,000 of dividends not being subject to tax, but unfortunately this does not extend the existing basic rate tax band.

The most comprehensive example given by HMRC is as follows

"I have a non-dividend income of £40,000, and receive dividends of £9,000 outside of an ISA" Of the £40,000 non-dividend income, £11,000 is covered by the Personal Allowance, leaving £29,000 to be taxed at basic rate.

This leaves £3,000 of income that can be earned within the basic rate limit before the higher rate threshold is crossed. The Dividend Allowance covers this £3,000 first, leaving £2,000 of Allowance to use in the higher rate band. All of this £5,000 dividend income is therefore covered by the Allowance and is not subject to tax.

The remaining £4,000 of dividends are all taxed at higher rate (32.5%).

Got it?

It just proves that it's not an increase in the nil rate band but the introduction of a stealth tax.

In 2015/16 Gibson was paid a salary of £10,000 by his company Gibson Ltd and voted a dividend of £30,000. Because of the tax credit attached to the dividend there will be no further tax to pay.

Compare this to 2016/17: same income levels, but his tax bill will now be £1,875 (£30,000 less £5,000 (free dividend allowance) @7.5%.

Very naughty Mr Osborne as this is typically how profits are extracted from most small family companies. Pay your partner the same amount and you've a tax bill of £3,750 whereas before you had no tax to pay! So you can see he's forcing you to consider moving into a limited company and then he'll tax the way you extract income from the company.

It has long been the practice for sole traders and partnerships to save income tax and National Insurance by incorporating and then paying dividends out of the profits and a salary up to the

National Insurance threshold as above. On relatively moderate profits this enables a husband and wife business to extract nearly £80,000 in a very tax efficient manner as indicated above.

For more worked examples see chapter 6 of Legally Avoid Property Taxes www.iainwallis.com/booksale.

The question though is above what level of profit is it worth incorporating and paying dividends? There are several useful ready reckoner tables online and like most accountants we have a spreadsheet that crunches the numbers. For businesses with profits below about £40,000, the administrative costs may outweigh the savings, though there are many views as to what the tip-over amount may be and certainly with the interest rate rule changes that figure could be much lower. Other tax matters associated with a company, such as provision of benefits, school fees etc. will also need to be factored in, but for me the biggest consideration should be the potential to shelter future capital growth within your property portfolio. So initially incorporation may be a sledgehammer to crack a nut, but if the protection of capital growth is factored in then it may be worthwhile.

For businesses with profits above the level for which incorporation remains beneficial, the issue is therefore how much more tax will be paid if the present level of dividends continue to be paid and is that a better result than paying a bonus instead? Paying a bonus will attract National Insurance, so for the moment dividends are always preferable to a bonus.

So how will this impact with those wrestling with the incorporation debate?

For those with modest profits (say less than £40,000) as I say it may initially be a sledgehammer to crack the nut, but above £40,000 it may be seen as advantageous. Those paying all profits as a dividend will see the advantage reduce, but if profits can be retained in the company the choice of whether to pay tax above the 20% corporation tax rate rests in the hands of the individual. Again, for those happy to retain company profits taxed at 20% for portfolio expansion, the dividend issue may be of less consequence. Increasingly I'm working with investors who have no need for the money and are happy for the profits to be retained in the company for future acquisitions.

For those with existing companies at the simplest level, dividends could be reduced to keep them all, along with taxable income, within the basic rate band. For some that may be enough to live on. As an alternative method of withdrawal maybe profit funds could be used to pay more towards pensions, though maybe like me, you plough all available funds into property as that is your pension.

You may have an existing company and could consider emptying the coffers! A dividend paid before 5 April 2016 should avoid the new surcharge. This advances tax payments for individuals and increases current tax take. There are particular circumstances in which it may be beneficial to consider this strategy.

Among issues to consider are, does the company have enough distributable reserves, the cash flow for the business and whether having cash from dividends, which thereby becomes chargeable assets for inheritance tax, may be a concern. This may especially be the case when paid by a company whose shares may attract business property relief. So let's explain that further.

If you've a company that's awash with cash, so long as it's a trading company i.e. developing property and not holding investment property, shares in that company will attract Business Property Relief and thus fall out of your estate for Inheritance Tax purposes. So if you paid a large divided to beat the 2015/16 changes that would then put cash into your bank account, which may be exposed to Inheritance Tax. The current nil rate band is £325,000 which could easily be eaten up by the value of your main home, though see the next section on the new RNRB.

It may be tempting to spread share ownership more widely within the family both to increase the number of individuals obtaining the benefit of both the £5,000 exemption and additional basic rate tax bands. Any sibling over 18 could be given shares and used to extract profits, but be careful! Do you want to dilute control of the company, which you will do by giving them voting shares in your company. So maybe look at issuing non voting B shares that can be used to extract profits, though again that income will be theirs and not yours!

Chapter 7

Inheritance Tax: Big Picture

When deciding whether to incorporate clearly you need to consider the impact of CGT, SDLT and funding issues. These are the three largest issues and the ones you need to get your head around first, but ask yourself this, why are you buying property and what do you want to be as your lasting legacy?

It may be that you've no kids in which case to die with £5,000,000 worth of property and £4,500,000 worth of debt is not an issue providing your rent roll finances the mortgage repayments and of course you will no longer get as much tax relief on the borrowings, so your tax bill will go up!

But what if you've children or even grandchildren: spending your life creating wealth is great, but not if when you go bang 40% goes straight off to HMRC in Inheritance Tax. It's a fact that most people spend their entire life trying to accumulate a reasonable amount of wealth, to take care of themselves in their old age and then pass on any remaining surplus to their children or even grandchildren.

It is somewhat unjust – or indeed downright wrong – that without careful planning and yes in certain cases a great deal of action throughout your life, then many families will ultimately face a huge and, frankly, unnecessary Inheritance Tax bill.

Now clearly if you are no more, you won't actually be writing the cheque payable to HMRC – but your estate will be paying Inheritance Tax on its overall value, be that your own home, your property portfolio, shares, cash at bank and valuables within the house. In certain cases that may mean selling property simply to pay the taxman!

Do you remember the opening lines of this book? If you do, then fantastic. The pain of paying unnecessary tax is still with you and, throughout this book, you've been noting where you've been leaving money with HMRC – and just what you will be doing in the future.

If you don't, then flick back now and remind yourself of what happened and how bad the pain was.

With the nil rate band currently £325,000, then most people can safely leave everything they have to their spouse or civil partner free from any Inheritance Tax plus, if you have no other dependants or potential beneficiaries to care about (and simply resent paying any unnecessary tax), you can simply leave it all to charity.

However, in the real world, most people do have someone they care about. Usually they have children or other family or friends whom they want to see benefit from the assets that they have built up in their lifetime; they don't want to see the government taking 40% of it away.

The mere fact that you are reading this book means that you are not like most people. Indeed, you are extraordinary because, like me, you are investing in property. Maybe to increase your passive income, maybe to create wealth for your retirement – or indeed any number of reasons. Wherever you are on this property journey and no matter what age you are Inheritance Tax will be around the corner somewhere. If you are young and entrepreneurial, then it may impact on your parents or grandparents; you have a responsibility to flag up the problems they may face.

If you are parents, then you need to be thinking about protecting your wealth and passing it to your children – and what about the impact on *your* parents? If you are in your twilight years well, how do you protect your hard-earned wealth and pass it to your children and their children?

It really is never too early – or indeed too late – to start planning.

Ever wondered why Inheritance Tax is called a voluntary tax?

Using a limited company to hold the properties offers excellent planning opportunities. Whilst the shares in a property investment company won't on their own save Inheritance Tax, with careful planning the shares can be removed from your estate for IHT purposes, while you continue to enjoy the income from those properties and decide which to hold and which to sell.

The purpose is to enable family wealth to be used to provide long-term benefits to children and grandchildren as a reward for working in the family investment business, rather than just 'handing over' the assets to them. Handing over the assets means a) you lose control of them and the income they produce and b) that family wealth will be weakened or even lost if the son or daughter falls in with the wrong crowd, gets married and then divorced! It also allows accumulated family wealth to be retained by the family for the long term and, therefore, allows it to be used flexibly to benefit children and grandchildren in the future.

It may be particularly suitable where there is a desire to prevent the next generation from dissipating family wealth, or to protect it from children's or grandchildren's spouses in the event of divorce or separation, so I sometimes refer to it as an "errant boyfriend or girlfriend trust"!

It enables control to be retained over the family wealth by the individual until succession, and thereafter to control how family wealth is applied to future generations. In addition, the family wealth is also largely protected from dissipation via future Inheritance Tax charges.

Essentially the process is as follows:

- Transfer value out of estate to a limited company
- Transfer a minimum of 50% of the shares in the company to some form of employee succession trust
- Obtain immediate 100% relief from IHT
- No need for a seven-year survival
- Continue to control the assets and the income

Yes there may be some SDLT, potential Capital Gains Tax and funding considerations to consider as outlined above, but these are significantly outweighed by the considerable savings. If you would like further information about this low risk and highly effective strategy please email iain@iainwallis.com.

Having your own limited company also enables other large costs (think school and university fees) to be paid through a company. Yes there are related income tax issues and as ever it's important to get the structures right, but the overall savings can be considerable.

With average university tuition fees and living costs now exceeding £18,000 per annum and private school fees typically around £12,000 per annum, the pre-tax cost of funding the education costs of our children is becoming ever more expensive.

An additional rate taxpayer will require over £100,000 of gross income over a three-year degree course simply to fund the education costs of their offspring. What that means is the company has to generate £125,000 of pre-tax company profits.

Funding 15 years of private education will require a staggering £255,000, which will require the company to generate nearly £320,000 in profit. Just how hard will you and the company have to work to generate those profits?

We can advise you on relatively straightforward planning techniques that can be utilised by the owners of family businesses to significantly reduce the tax suffered on the income needed to meet those costs through our bespoke school fees planning.

The planning is available to any owner-managed business owner with children at school or about to attend university. It also works with grandparents looking to assist with school fees for their grandchildren. It is not aggressive, not disclosable under the DoTAS regime, and unaffected by the General Anti-Abuse Rule.

As with succession planning if this is of interest please email iain@iainwallis.com.

Chapter 8

Residence Nil Rate Band

On 1 October 2007 the BBC reported from the Conservative party conference that George Osborne in his conference speech said that *"The threshold for Inheritance Tax would rise from £300,000 to £1m under a Conservative government"*.

Well better late than never George, for what he actually did was freeze the nil rate band (the amount before IHT bites at 40%) at £325,000 in October 2009 and it's still at this level today 2016/17! So a little smoke and mirrors and an election pledge or two later he has delivered: or has he?

Whilst the headline figure is very impressive, could he just not have sprinkled "Elsa" (trust me I had to look this up!) like dust on the **frozen** nil rate band and simply indexed it up for inflation?

The Residence Nil Rate Band (RNRB) will be in addition to the standard nil rate band of £325,000. It will take the form of an extra amount that can be offset against the value of property (or possibly assets representing it) that has, at some point, been occupied as a residence. It is available when that residence is transferred, usually on the death of the owner to their direct descendants.

The amount of the person's estate, over and above any RNRB and standard nil rate band to which they may be entitled, is charged at the normal rates that apply for Inheritance Tax. For married couples and civil partners, the nil rate band entitlement on second death will include any transferable standard nil rate band or carried forward RNRB that was not used when the first person died.

The RNRB will take effect on deaths on or after 6 April 2017.

As the proposed legislation stands, the RNRB applies only to people who have children or grandchildren. Because of this there are, not unnaturally, a group of childless couples who may just wish to leave their house to other relatives.

The additional RNRB will be available if all or part of a "qualifying residential interest" is "closely inherited" on or after 6 April 2017. What you may well ask is a qualifying residential interest? And the answer is "a dwelling house which has at any time been the deceased's residence and which forms part of the deceased's estate".

It would therefore exclude a property that has always been a buy to let, but could include a property that has, in the past, been a residence of the deceased, but which was let at the date of death. Indeed, it would seem that it could apply to a valuable property acquired and occupied as a residence by the deceased shortly before death with that person having previously always lived in rented accommodation.

The RNRB will be phased in gradually between 6 April 2017 and 6 April 2020 on the following basis:

- £100,000 for 2017/18
- £125,000 for 2018/19
- £150,000 for 2019/20
- £175,000 for 2020/21

From 6 April 2021, the RNRB will increase in line with the consumer price index.

The RNRB will be only be available when an owner dies on or after 6 April 2017 and the family home is transferred, generally on death, to the direct descendants of the deceased. A direct descendant is a child (including step-child, adopted child or foster child) and grandchild. A guardian appointed to act on behalf of a minor is also treated for these purposes as a direct descendant.

In general, the transfer to the direct descendant must be outright, but some other transfers on death into trust for the benefit of those descendants are permitted. These include:

- transfers into bare trusts
- transfers into immediate post-death interest trusts; and
- transfers into 18 to 25 trusts and trusts for bereaved minors

Although the new rules do not come fully into effect until 6 April 2017, you should still take them into account when planning, using wills and lifetime gifts, or at least your solicitor should!

Bear in mind that you might own two or more properties which might all qualify for the RNRB, so thought needs to be given to when those properties are left to children or grandchildren and the need to make an election to obtain the maximum relief.

If one of a married couple is in serious ill health and plans to leave a qualifying residence worth more than £325,000 to children or grandchildren on death before 6 April 2017, this strategy should be reviewed because no RNRB would be available and so Inheritance Tax would arise (whereas the transferable nil rate band could be available to the survivor).

Conversely if it is likely that one spouse will die before 6 April 2017, but the other will survive past that date, the first to die could leave a share of the private residence to children or grandchildren on the first death (within the standard nil rate band) because the survivor will obtain a full 100% transferable RNRB. Much depends on the full circumstances of the case.

Certain arrangements in wills should be reviewed to ensure that none of the RNRB is wasted. For example:

- If a private residence is owned in tenancy in common by spouses with a view to the share of the first to die passing to a discretionary will trust, this arrangement should be reviewed to make sure that none of the RNRB is wasted either on the first death or on the death of a survivor.

- When the first person of a couple to die sets up a nil rate band discretionary will trust, where the legacy can be satisfied by a charge on residential property passing to the survivor, thought will need to be given to whether this will have an impact on the availability of the carry-forward allowance on the surviving spouse's death. It may be that the introduction of the RNRB will result in more people abandoning nil rate band discretionary will trusts.

- It is not unusual for parents to want assets to pass into trust for their children after the surviving spouse's death, for asset protection reasons. However, the RNRB will not be available if assets pass into a discretionary trust, even if the beneficiaries of that trust are limited to lineal descendants. Yet, if assets pass on trusts that create an immediate post-death interest, a disabled person's interest, an 18 to 25 trust or one for bereaved minors, the RNRB is available.

According to the Royal Institution of Chartered Surveyors, property prices are set to increase over the next five years by 25%. So, even if a house is below the combined nil rate band threshold now, it may not be in the future. If house price inflation exceeds CPI, more estates with property will fall into the Inheritance Tax net.

In short, the introduction of the RNRB is another good reason to review existing wills.

Finally, and this is just my take on this, but does it make sense for homes, as opposed to estates in general, to be singled out for special treatment? Most children sell the parental home after the surviving parent's death to divide the estate between them. If the RNRB is just a means for children to retain more funds after tax to pay the mortgages on their own homes, why not keep it simple and increase the standard nil rate band with house price inflation each year instead? That however doesn't give election winning headlines though!

Summary

This subtitle to this book is "What's George up to?" and by now you've hopefully got a greater understanding of the challenges that you face and some of the options to consider.

For me the key thing is not to panic, bury your head in the sand or think that this is the end of the BTL world as we know it. Yes there are some major challenges ahead and if it was easy everybody else would be doing it. If you think you can deal with them you will do, if you think that you can't then you won't. As that saying goes, whether you think you can or you can't, you're right!

Don't be among the ones who can't!

You've faced challenges before and dealt with them and this onslaught is no different. Remember the fear of buying your first BTL property, but you dealt with it.

So take stock of where you are, what you've achieved and what else you would like to achieve in the world of property.

Trite as it may be, make a plan and work it.

Yes there's plenty more fuel on the fire about using a limited company and as ever you now know, as you did having read the first book, "it depends".

There are challenges ahead with CGT SDLT and finance. Know how big those challenges are and what can be done to mitigate them before proceeding. For some short term pain for massive long term gain is a one off cost. Yes that may need financing either through restructuring existing debt or selling stock to release capital. In five years' time you may be looking back wishing that you had formed a company ages ago.

So ask yourself these simple questions:

1.   Do you have a BTL portfolio?
2.   Do you have concerns about the tax changes?
3.   Do you need guidance on the changes?
4.   Are you concerned about the impact of capital taxes?
5.   Is your estate worth more than £325,000?
6.   Do you want the peace of mind that you're running a tax efficient portfolio?

If you answered 'yes' to more than three of the above questions then I would suggest you need our Property Portfolio Tax Audit because your hard earned wealth is exposed to tax.

Our simple to understand audit will help you preserve your wealth.

3 simple steps to peace of mind:

1.   You complete our initial Fact Find document and return to us.
2.   We'll phone you to discuss initial recommendations and tax challenges.
3.   You will have a personal consultation to discuss recommendations in greater detail and help you implement a bespoke action plan.

Can you afford not to undertake a Property Portfolio Tax Audit to protect your wealth and provide peace of mind and a lasting legacy?

Alternatively book a consultation with me. It will be unique, tailored to your specific challenges and specific needs and as with everything we do comes with our 100% money back guarantee. If you'd like to book a strategic consultation please email iain@iainwallis.com.

Finally can I impose on your good nature? If this book has been helpful to you, I would really appreciate you leaving a review where you purchased it and/or here https://www.goodreads.com/ along with sharing on social media with the # #sharetheknowledge and #savethetax

If you then email me iain@iainwallis.com a link to your review I will send you a bonus Taxability Checklist for 2016/17 sharing over 60 ways that you can save more tax.

Thank you for investing in this book and then investing the time to read it and may it enable you to make choices for your continued and successful property investing.

Thanks

This has to start with thanks to Dad and Mum.

Though he's no longer here, for he died far too young at 65, Dad's values and beliefs live on through me and my younger brother Julian. Although it was not until Apollo 13 that we heard the phrase "failure is not an option", Dad practised it every day; he created not one, but two successful manufacturing companies, both started in different recessions. Was it tough for him? You bet, so please never use a recession as a reason as to why you can't make money in your business.

Cheers Dad – and it's a real shame that you are not around to see that, though we had a few scrapes along the way, your sons both did alright in the end.

Thanks, Mum, for always being there to pick us up when we fell over – and always having a "yes, you can" attitude.

You can choose your friends but not your family and in Julian, my younger brother, I have the best of both worlds. Sure, there's been some sibling rivalry but he's a true friend and trusted partner. We speak daily, whether to discuss last night's football or some business matter; I count myself lucky to have such a great relationship with him. He has completely smashed the 'Father, Son, Bankrupt' myth and runs a very sound ship that Dad would have been immensely proud of, as indeed am I. So, thanks Jules who along with Marcie his wife have always proved good council.

Finally, and by no means last, all this would not be possible – or indeed worthwhile – without the love and support of Fenella. I have no doubt that sometimes it can't be easy being married to a Wallis, but your chirpiness and loving smile always shine through. You are the peas to my carrots, Jenny to Forest Gump, and I love you loads.

Thank you for making me laugh at least once a day – along with keeping Blandford, Douglas and Fraser, not forgetting the irrepressible Sweep, in order.

Iain Wallis FCA April 2016

Also by Iain Wallis

Legally Avoid Property Taxes: 51 Top Tips to Save Property Taxes & Increase your Wealth

Verified Amazon Reviews

"A really useful book for every property investor. I like to think I already know a lot about how to minimise tax in relation to property but I picked up some really valuable tips and was reminded of things that I knew but was not using. The information in this book is priceless. As an investor we need to know not only how to make money but how to keep as much of that money as possible. This book will help you keep more of the money you make and you may want to give this book to your accountant who may not know as much about property tax as Iain knows. I highly recommend this." **Simon Zutshi**

"This is an excellent, practical book. It is very readable, with lots of worked examples helping to illustrate points." **J Gray**

"I have often steered clear of books offering financial guidance but it is a delight to read a book that is in clear language, offers good advice and is free from the jargon some accountants revel in" **S White**

"He clearly knows his stuff and this book has already saved me over £5,000 in allowable expenses that I was blissfully unaware of". **N Willis**

"I am pleased to say that his mischievous humour and skilled presentation have translated to the book as well as the speaker platform. He knows how to build up the information and present it in bite size chunks, so that he keeps the reader engaged" **S Green**

"Certainly NOT a dull book full of accounting jargon. All aspects are explained using case stories and clear English". **Desi**

"Iain Wallis really knows his stuff (vital info on avoiding property taxes, claiming what is legally allowed) and explains it in a clear, entertaining and succinct way. Really like the use of case studies throughout the book too. A *must buy* for all property investors and entrepreneurs like us!" **V Grace**

"You won't get a better book than this on property taxes". **S Harvey**

"Simply-written book about what is one of the most traditionally boring subjects – taxes. Iain keeps the reader engaged with not only valuable information about how the UK tax system works in respect to property, but also includes helpful tips dispersed throughout the book" **T Riby Williams**

Available here www.iainwallis.com/booksale

Printed in Great Britain
by Amazon